GIRLS IN GREEN

A PORTRAIT OF ST HELEN'S, NORTHWOOD

GIRLS IN GREEN

A PORTRAIT OF ST HELEN'S, NORTHWOOD

Edited by Kate Ogden and Susan Millership

First published in 2009 by
Third Millennium Publishing Limited,
a subsidiary of Third Millennium Information Limited.

2–5 Benjamin Street
London
United Kingdom
EC1M 5QL
www.tmiltd.com

ISBN 978 1 906507 10 7

Edited by Kate Ogden and Susan Millership
Designed by Susan Pugsley
Production by Bonnie Murray
Reprographics by Studio Fasoli, Italy
Printed by Gorenjski Tisk, Slovenia

Cover image: Charles Best www.charlesbest.co.uk

ACKNOWLEDGEMENTS

The school would like to thank all the Old Girls, staff past and present, and
current pupils who have contributed to this book. We have used as many
of your contributions as has been possible and all contributions will form a
valuable and fascinating contribution to the school archives. Much material
in the book has come from the archives and the assistance of Gillian Hill and
Teresa Betts has been invaluable. We would also like to thank Rosalind Onians
and all the Old Girls who contributed to 'St Helen's: The First Eighty Years'
as this publication has provided a wonderful source of early memories and
information. We are extremely grateful for all the time and effort put into
the book by everyone who has been involved and, in particular, to Joanna
Chaventré, Sally Fleming, Rebecca Hershman, Mary Morris and Mary Rose
Seldon who have been on hand throughout the process of putting 'Girls in
Green' together to offer their advice, and also to Rebecca Clarke who helped
source information and scan in countless photographs. Most images come
from the School Archive. The publishers and St Helen's would like to thank
the following for providing additional images: Teresa Betts, Kim Fishman,
Neil Flash, Sally Fleming, Miles Gillman, Elizabeth Grant, Rebecca Hershman,
Christine Janis, Suzanne King, Janet Kirchheimer, Sarah Kirchheimer, June
Leader, Rosemary McLure, Fiona Mook-Dewey, Natasha Rodikis Presvytis, Mrs
J Rudge, Mary Rose Seldon, Jessica Sims, Beryl Taylor. We have tried to use as
many of the images provided as possible. Thanks also go to Michael Gosling
and Paul Kilvington, some of whose photographs have been reproduced in this
book and also to Mary Evans Picture Library for the map on p17 and Interfoto/
Alamy for the photograph on p54.

Although every reasonable effort has been made to identify copyright
holders of images used in this book, any further information will be welcomed
by the publishers.

Contents

Old Girls' maiden names are given in brackets with their year of leaving.

Foreword

As St Helen's celebrates its 110th year, I feel privileged to be able to share in the life of a school that has such a strong sense of community. Its founder, May Rowland Brown, was a woman of strong Christian principles with a clear vision for her school, a vision which was shared by her sisters, her mother and one of her cousins who all supported the development of St Helen's in one way or another in the early years of its history. The ethos and values that they fostered in the school are still very much alive today, a testament to the headmistresses, and others, who have left their mark and developed St Helen's into the lively, thriving and diverse community that it is today.

This is not a complete history of the school; rather it is a celebration of the life of the school and the experience of being a part of the St Helen's community, both past and present, told through fascinating and entertaining memories and anecdotes. A huge amount of material was sent in from Old Girls, current pupils, and staff past and present, and as much has been included as was possible. This book also owes a great deal to the huge wealth of material in the school archives as well as *St Helen's: The First Eighty Years*, compiled by Old Girl Rosalind Onians, from which many early memories have been drawn.

St Helen's in the twenty-first century is a school that has a strong sense of its past and a clear vision for its future within the global community. Over its history, society in general and women's education in particular, has changed dramatically and St Helen's has readily adapted to these changes with innovative style. Today, as always, St Helen's girls leave with a strong sense of self, ready and willing to take on the challenges of the adult world and part of an incredibly strong community of Old Girls who are proud to have been one of the 'girls in green'.

ROSIE FAUNCH, CHAIRMAN OF THE COUNCIL OF GOVERNORS
JULY 2009

Traditions and Legacy

Gillian Hill

Alice May Rowland Brown, known as May, was the eldest of the five daughters of a London printer. The early history of St Helen's is also the history of this woman and her family; from 1899 to 1945 the story of the school is inextricably bound up with the lives of May Rowland Brown, her mother, her sisters and one of her cousins. It was May whose visionary faith and respect for education gave the school its start, and who saw it grow and prosper under her loving care. Her mother's organisational abilities provided support for the vision, and later the complementary interests and skills of her sisters, Doris and Beatrice, led the school along the path that saw it become an independent school after World War Two.

In 1893 a new boarding school for girls opened in Northwood. It had begun life in London, but the owners had chosen to move it to the countryside, where it was renamed Northwood College; it opened in Maxwell Road with 20 boarders and two day-pupils. May Rowland Brown, fresh from her studies at the Cambridge Training College for Women, started work there that year. She was clearly a capable and popular teacher, strongly influenced by the founder and first Principal of the Cambridge Training College, Miss E P Hughes. Tradition has it that Northwood College took only 'the daughters of gentlemen' and refused to take the daughters of anyone associated with trade. It also was primarily a boarding school at this time, and there was a growing number of girls in the area needing to be educated. In 1898, Miss Rowland Brown, then 25 years old and with only five years' teaching experience, was approached by three local businessmen and asked if she would set up a school for day-pupils in Northwood.

It is unlikely that May Rowland Brown had expected to be a headmistress by the age of 25. She was initially reluctant, but her upbringing had taught her not to fear responsibility. She prayed for guidance, and then accepted the task with growing enthusiasm.

The Rowland Brown Family: (standing L-R) Charles, May, Doris, Ethel; (seated L-R) Beatrice, Alice, Hilda.

Opposite: Form IV in the early 1900s.

The Rowland Brown Family – *Gillian Hill (Archivist)*

Initially, the Rowland Browns were simply the Brown family. Charles Rowland Brown was born in 1836, the third son of a London doctor, Thomas Brown. In 1869 he married Alice Rolfe, who came from a long line of landed gentry and clergymen, and had grown up in the parish of St Helen's, Bishopsgate. Between 1873 and 1880 they had five daughters, four of whom were given Rowland as an additional forename.

In 1885, while the children were still young, Mr Brown's printing business ran into difficulties. Mrs Brown, a practical and resourceful woman, was determined to see her daughters did not suffer because of family financial problems. She was ambitious for her daughters, and aware of the disadvantages of being a female in the late Victorian era. They all received a good education, sound religious training, an awareness of duty and responsibility to others, and a grounding in practical household skills. It was a time when marriage and a family were the usual expectations for young women, but until then they had to earn their own livings. Against this backdrop, the sisters all became teachers until they married.

In about 1890 Charles and his elder brother, Edwin, both began to use double-barrelled surnames. Charles became Mr Rowland Brown, and Edwin, Burton-Brown. His daughter Constance played an important part in the early days of the school. The sisters were known simply as Brown in childhood, but by the time May was teaching at Northwood College in 1893 she was known by the new version.

The printing business recovered, but before long Mr Rowland Brown retired. He and his wife then moved to Northwood, where he died in 1905. His widow devoted the rest of her life to the school her eldest daughter had founded, and was known as 'The Mother of St Helen's'.

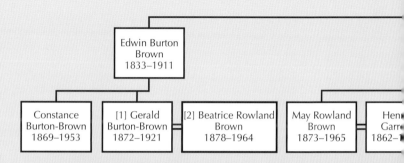

The Rowland Brown Family with Ethel's husband, John Cavenagh (pictured standing in centre).

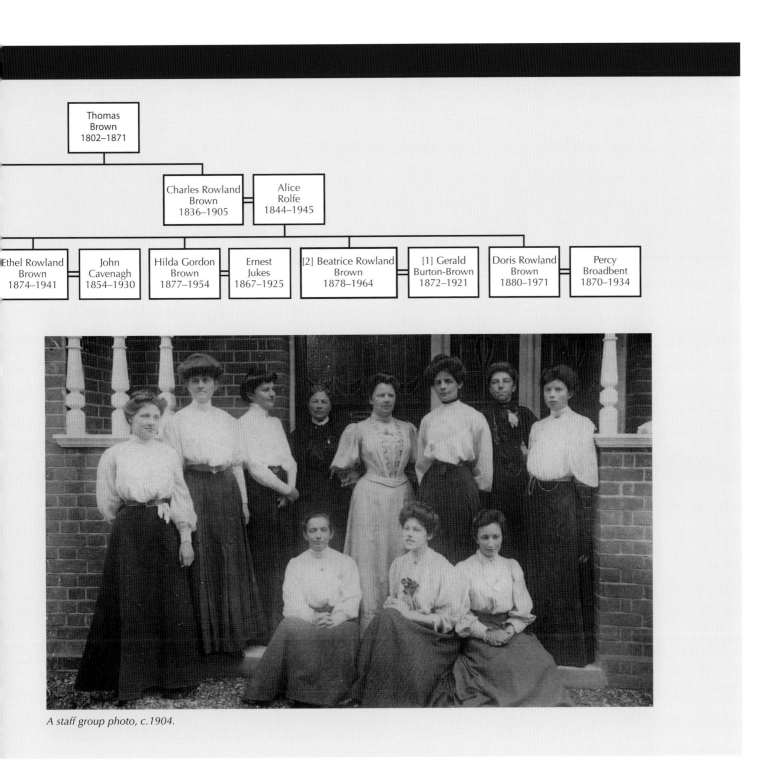

A staff group photo, c.1904.

Miss Doris and Percy Broadbent on their wedding day, 1913.

to stay at St Helen's. So during term-time the couple lived apart, she in Northwood and he in Guildford. She would visit him at half-term and weekends.

With the outbreak of World War One in 1914, Miss Rowland Brown organised the girls to provide as much practical help as possible for the war effort. Belgian refugees were given a temporary home at St Helen's, and Miss Doris's French was invaluable. Mount Vernon Hospital housed many wounded soldiers, and groups of girls would help or entertain them. Eva Seldon (Morley, 1926) remembered: 'Some of the convalescent soldiers would come over to the school to play cricket with the girls. All of us were busy knitting socks and Balaclava helmets for the soldiers and sailors.' In the holidays, some older girls helped on farms – weeding, potato-picking and hay-making.

St Helen's Boys

When St Helen's was founded, its first 12 pupils included some of the girls' brothers. A few boys continued to attend the school as young day-pupils, before moving on to boys' schools which started at a slightly older age, until 1981 when a local school, St Martin's, opened a class for rising fives. A book about St Helen's would be incomplete without some Old Boys' memories.

The presence of boys added another dimension to school life as Sir Oliver Popplewell (1933) recalls: 'My main recollection is being in a gang with a boy called Keith and we frightened the girls with pea-shooters.' Jonathan Mundy (1976) remembers: 'One of the best things was being taught football by Dr Laycock whose enthusiasm gave me a love for the game later on.'

Neil Flash (1980) recalls his time at St Helen's fondly: 'I clearly remember my classroom in what is now the Little Gables building, the playing field next to it where we were taught football and the little wooden Wendy house in the playground into which we used to chase the girls!'

Group of boys in the early 1900s and Neil Flash, 1980 (top right).

The Hoxton Mission

Described in 1966 by Miss Mackenzie as the school's 'first charitable event', the pupils and Old Girls of St Helen's supported the poor living in Hoxton for many years. Starting in the early years of the school's history, there was an annual all-day working party during the Christmas term, where staff and girls would produce clothes which were sent to St John's Church of England School in Hoxton.

Another almost annual event was the summer garden party at the school, when the elderly, mothers and babies of Hoxton would be invited to the school for the day. Violet Slade Jones wrote in 1925 that, 'Mr. Lloyd writes in a letter thanking Mrs. Broadbent for entertaining a number of mothers at St. Helen's last June, "The mothers were charmed with their visit to St. Helen's. All through the dark days of winter, June 25th will shine through the gloom of their surroundings. After last year and in the darkest days the phrase – there's Northwood coming – would bring a smile of hope." I imagine it – the memory of one day at St. Helen's, and we fortunate people who have the memory of hundreds!'

In the mid-1920s, the school's relationship with the Hoxton poor developed further with the adoption of a Mission connected with St John's Church which became known as the 'St Helen's Mission'. School magazines show that several Old Girls were heavily involved with supporting the Mission, raising money for the Mission Hall's rent, giving their time to improve the rooms and organising Christmas parties. Deaconess Gladys Murch, the first pupil of St Helen's, was heavily involved with helping the poor in this area of east London and in leading the Mission. In 1936, the work of the Mission moved to the parish of St Bartholomew, Islington, a parish that Deaconess Murch had worked in previously.

This spirit of giving time and money to help others is one that has most certainly lived on in future generations of St Helen's girls.

'One of the things we learned is that we were the lucky ones and we had to do things for the less fortunate in this world. A lot of the people I know do, or have done, a certain amount of voluntary work.'

FELICITY YUILLE (WEST, 1947)

The school continued to grow. By 1919, after 20 years, there were 162 pupils, one third of whom were boarders. The aim of the school was 'the provision of a thoroughly efficient training which shall develop the character and personality of each pupil'. There was no pressure to achieve academic success; by now about two girls a year would go on to university, and the principals were certainly very proud of them, but they were more concerned that their pupils should grow into responsible adults. They believed very strongly in the strength and independence of women, but accepted that for many of them a home and family would still be of great importance, and tried to instil qualities and values that would be useful whatever paths they took. Some would have a career before marriage. A number of the early pupils did not marry, but embarked on service as doctors, nurses, missionaries, teachers and charity workers around the world.

Boarders rarely went out, except in organised groups, and had to make their own amusements. Small groups would each week put on some kind of entertainment – a tea-party, a play, music, or organised games. A great deal of ingenuity and friendly rivalry went into these activities and invitations had to be formally delivered and correctly accepted.

By Easter 1922, Miss Rowland Brown was aware that the school needed more accommodation. Over the last few years both houses and fields nearby had been bought or rented, but the time had come for another building on the main site. She drew up plans for Middle House (now Gwyer), which was finished early in 1923.

'Words of encouragement, of warning, of correction told to a schoolgirl became immortal. "An intelligent person is never bored," said Mrs Broadbent to a thin coltish girl in 1924 who could not forget it.'

MARGARET MADDOCKS (COOPER, 1927)

Opposite: Fire drill, c.1906.

Calendar Sale – *Teresa Betts (Massey, 1961)*

The first Calendar Sale took place in the autumn of 1916. Miss Phillips, who taught Botany, had a particularly artistic Third Form, and their flower illustrations mounted on card with calendars attached were sold to endow a cot at the Canning Town Settlement. The sale was held in the school hall and £20 was raised. The sale became an annual event as more items were made and sold. In 1925 the proceeds totalled £170 and were divided amongst charities including the Church Missionary Society, Queen Mary's Hospital, Northwood Hospital, Hoxton Guides, British and Foreign Sailors Fund and the Waifs and Strays, as well as ten guineas for the school library. Between the wars, the afternoon always finished with a play.

Calendar Sale continued during World War Two in Northwood – Mrs Broadbent would come down from Wales to look after the stall for the Hoxton Mission.

In 1949 plans were announced for the building of the Rowland Brown Hall, which was to be opened in 1959 (the school's 60th birthday year), and Calendar Sales became bigger affairs to help raise money. Senior girls ran sideshows, providing fun whilst accumulating money in penny and tuppenny amounts. A 'Mile of Sixpences' was introduced, and fathers were urged to turn out their pockets for sixpences to see which House could have the longest line by the end of the day. The Old Girls took over from Mrs Broadbent running their own stall, with proceeds going directly to charities in which OGs took an active part in Britain and around the world. As the size of the school increased, two Calendar Sales were held each year, one for Junior School and Little St Helen's in October and one for the seniors after half term.

By 1989 it had become harder to fit two Calendar Sales into the available Saturdays, when there were so many sporting fixtures to be arranged as well as the end of term play. So the decision was taken to make one big event for the whole school. A Father Christmas Grotto was installed in the green rooms. It was very popular and younger children waited patiently to see Santa.

Calendar Sale is now organised by the school's Charities Co-ordinator, Jeanne Phillips: 'Calendar Sale continues to go from strength to strength. Every year the huge variety of stalls across the site raises in excess of £6,000 for a host of charities. The most impressive thing is the large number of girls wanting to set up and run many of the stalls for charities of their own choice. It is certainly an event in the true spirit of St Helen's in its commitment to raising money for charity.'

Calendar Sale is a tradition that the school can be proud of, as Rosalind Onians (Lathbury, 1934) said, 'it is the permanence of it'.

Calendar Sale in the Rowland Brown Hall, 1990s.

Middle House, 1929.

> '*I remember, in my first or second term, the excitement with which we received Miss Rowland Brown's news of her engagement to Mr Garrett, and the charm of her shyly proud gesture as she drew his portrait from her bosom.*'
>
> NANCY WITTS (SALZMAN, 1926)

In January 1923 Miss Rowland Brown took a short holiday in Sussex. While there she met a Mr Henry Garrett, a widower with four adult children. A year later they announced their engagement and on 11th April 1924 they were married at St Martin-in-the-Fields. They moved to a house in Frithwood Avenue, a short walk from the school. The new Mrs Garrett retired as headmistress, but continued to teach Scripture, and was a frequent visitor to the school; she and her husband would entertain groups of girls to tea at their home after hay-making. Mr Garrett was a reserved character who treated the girls with a charming, old-fashioned courtesy.

As one member of the family left, another replaced her. The fourth Rowland Brown sister, Beatrice, had studied Domestic Economy; she had then taught at the Northern Polytechnic in Holloway, but left when she married her cousin Gerald Burton-Brown, brother of Constance. Since then she had served on various associated committees, and became an Inspector of Domestic Subjects for the Board of Education. Her husband had died in 1921 and her only child, a daughter, was already at the school, so it seemed the obvious course for her to join Doris as

The Chalet School Connection
– Gillian Hill (Archivist)

In 1921 Miss Dyer, a typical 1920s spinster schoolmistress with untidy and baggy clothes, arrived to teach English to junior girls. She was a talented and popular teacher, but she stayed only two years. She went on to teach elsewhere, and then ran a school of her own. She was also a writer of school-based stories for girls.

She had started writing before she came to St Helen's, and her first school story was published while she was there. During the holidays she took a trip to the Austrian Tyrol, and this inspired 'The School at the Chalet' (1925) which was followed by many sequels. Although there are also many differences, her fictional Chalet School owes a great deal to St Helen's – in some of its customs and traditions, its names, and in its general atmosphere. Each school was founded with a handful of pupils by one young woman of strong character with a close family. In both schools the boarders in particular are treated as an extension of the family. The young headmistress's birthday is celebrated with presents and masses of flowers. In one book a new mistress introduces the idea of 'Spot Suppers' and the words of 'A spot on the table cloth' are supplied 'courtesy of Miss M Rowland Brown'. One of the pupils is called Hilda Jukes – the married name of 'Miss Hilda'. At St Helen's she expanded her surname from Dyer to the double-barrelled Brent-Dyer, as the Rowland Browns had done.

By the time she died in 1969 Elinor M Brent-Dyer had written 58 books in one of the most enduring series in children's literature.

Miss Dyer, 1922 (pictured top left).

The Burton-Brown Family: (L-R) Beatrice, Margaret, Gerald, Constance.

co-principal when Mrs Garrett left. She was a gentle person, of great charm, and was generally thought to be the best-looking of the sisters.

After her marriage Mrs Broadbent had continued to be known within the school as 'Miss Doris', but from now on she would be known as Mrs Broadbent. She stopped going to join her husband in Guildford at weekends; instead, he came to Northwood. Affectionately known as Uncle Percy, he was popular with the girls, and sometimes helped with the French lessons.

While Mrs Broadbent concentrated on the academic side, Mrs Burton-Brown's first move was to improve the domestic side of the school – she set about improving the school diet, and renovated the cloakrooms and kitchens. She also established an excellent Domestic Science course. Later, in 1938, Doris wrote to a friend that 'the present St Helen's is really Mrs Burton-Brown's creation' – Mrs Garrett had been a 'wonderful founder and figurehead', but Mrs Burton-Brown's energy and determination had been vital to the shaping of the school.

New School, joined to the main building by a loggia, opened in 1929. The school now extended south, leaving only a narrow pathway separating it from the orchard of the neighbouring house, Fitzwalters. The following year saw a very popular addition – the school's first swimming pool. Enthusiasm for cricket as a summer sport waned rapidly, as the state-of-the-art

Opposite: Evening Prep, 1931.

steam-heated pool became a major attraction. The pool also led to considerable publicity for the school with articles in magazines and newspapers.

'It was the caring by the Rowland Brown family for each and every child that made Little St Helen's a good place in which to spend those few impressionable years before the anxieties and perplexities of exams and adolescence intruded. Friendships lasting more than 50 years were formed there and the roots of service and responsibility were planted in that far away "Age of Innocence".'

Isabel Pearson (Drummond, 1933)

Daphne Blundell CB

Daphne Blundell joined St Helen's in 1925. After leaving school in 1934, Daphne trained and worked in social services before joining the Women's Royal Naval Service (WRNS) during World War Two. She rose steadily as an officer and became Director of the WRNS, for which she was awarded the honour of CB in 1972.

When she retired from service, she became President of the Association of the WRNS and was a Governor of St Helen's from 1970 until 1995. As a Governor, Dr Yvonne Burne remembers that 'She was always fair, objective, sensible and understanding. Her sense of the school's needs and her knowledge of what was required for its development and direction made a wise Governor, whom I greatly admired and liked.'

Not only did she devote much of her time to the school, but also to the community of Northwood, supporting activities at Holy Trinity Church and as Chairman of James House, the Abbeyfield Home. Daphne was committed to public service, as Mary Rose Seldon (1947) described in the 2004 *Old Girls' Magazine*: 'One of our most distinguished OGs, loved and respected by a wide variety of people across the country, quiet, unassuming, totally to be relied upon, always ready with a wise and considered judgement, and, at the right moment, a twinkle.'

Dom Econ – *Gillian Hill*

Domestic Science Room, c.1910.

As in all but the most academic of girls' schools, household skills were part of the curriculum from an early stage. Cookery, needlework and general housekeeping were often collectively given a grander name, and in 1910 St Helen's acquired a dedicated Domestic Science room, above the new multi-purpose hall.

This suited immediate needs, but when Mrs Burton-Brown arrived as co-principal in 1924 she wanted to expand. Domestic Economy was her speciality, and she felt 'a comprehensive course should be introduced as soon as possible to bring Home Science to the same standard as the rest of the educational scheme'. She set about creating such a course, very advanced for its time, and had a small bungalow built in the school grounds as a teaching aid. Beyond the kitchens, on a site where chickens had been kept during World War One, it was originally designated 'The Home Science Pavilion' but rapidly became generally known as 'Dom Econ'.

Domestic Science, 1930s.

It was fitted out with every modern convenience. There was a kitchen with gas, electric and solid fuel cookers; a scullery and sitting room; and upstairs a bedroom and bathroom. For several years Miss Crawford presided over it, and Mrs Burton-Brown would lecture on Home Management, Hygiene and Dietetics. Each year a dozen or so sixth formers without academic ambitions would take an intensive course in all aspects of practical housewifery, including dressmaking, millinery, sewing-machine maintenance and baby-care.

With the outbreak of World War Two, the specialised course had to stop, although domestic science teaching continued in one form or another until the 1990s. The bungalow survived long enough to be dwarfed by the Rowland Brown Hall in 1959, but was demolished in the early 1960s to allow for completion of the quad.

Housewifery: window cleaning, 1932.

Cookery lesson, 1985.

Dom Econ next to the Rowland Brown Hall, 1961.

The Percy Broadbent pavilion in use, 2009.

By mid-1934 Mrs Garrett was 61, and Mrs Broadbent and Mrs Burton-Brown were in their mid-fifties. The principals were planning to give up running the school, and were making plans both for the school's future and for their own. Mrs Garrett visited the school regularly, teaching Scripture and Art, but was no longer so closely involved. Their mother, Mrs Rowland Brown, was approaching 90; she was planning to move to a flat in central London, and Mrs Burton-Brown was going to leave the school to look after her. Percy Broadbent was due to retire at Christmas, and Doris planned to retire soon afterwards.

To secure the future of St Helen's as an Independent Public School, a Council of Governors was appointed and its duties were to be mainly advisory. The sisters, accustomed to pursuing policy themselves, frequently acted without consulting it, particularly when prompt action was needed to secure property for the school.

In December 1934 Mr Broadbent died suddenly, and Mrs Broadbent decided to stay on as headmistress. A replacement had already been appointed; a joint headship was proposed, but the successful candidate obtained another headship. One of her first acts as headmistress was to build a sports pavilion in memory of her husband.

In 1935 Mrs Burton-Brown and Mrs Rowland Brown moved to London, but after living with their huge 'family' in the school they found central London strangely quiet and soon returned. They moved into one of the cottages in Rofant Road, a short walk

Opposite: The prefects' room, 1920s.

The House System

In the spring term of 1927, the introduction of a new House system was announced, with the aim of bringing day and boarding girls together and to encourage good work and behaviour through House loyalty. Three Houses were formed, two named after the Antarctic explorers Sir Ernest Shackleton and Captain Robert Scott, and the third after Brig. Gen. Charles Bruce, a distinguished Himalayan explorer.

House loyalty was encouraged from the outset and a points system was introduced to reward successes in areas of school life, including examinations, elocution, music and sports, and to punish misbehaviour. At the end of the school year, the name of the victorious House was inscribed on the new House shield, a gift from the first three House Captains.

The new House badges were worn with great pride and new House activities began, including inter-House sports matches, charity work and annual House picnics. 'Such delightful country spots as Juniper Hill, Oxhey Woods, Hamper Mill or Ruislip Reservoir were the usual venues for vigorous games of rounders, dramatic sketches, sing-songs and gargantuan teas. These occasions when staff and girls joined in the jollifications were enormously appreciated by everyone,' writes Rosalind Onians (Lathbury, 1934). In 1930 an Inter-House Competition in Music was introduced, later expanded to include Elocution, and an Art Competition was started a few years later.

The House system flourished and, in 1976, a fourth House accommodated the rapidly-increasing numbers in the school. June Leader recalled, 'Mrs Stewart suggested that Bonington would be a suitable name, in key with the achievements mirrored by Scott, Shackleton and Bruce, so with the public spirited secession from other Houses of a few seniors, especially Nicola Sandom and Vanessa Lawrence ... the fourth House was born'.

In 1999, Junior School introduced a separate House system. The idea of inspirational women was decided upon with pupils able to suggest names. Girls voted for the new House names from a shortlist: Curie (orange), Keller (turquoise) and Nightingale (magenta) were chosen, all great women in history.

from the school. Mrs Burton-Brown did not return to work, as she had to look after her mother, and many of her duties had already been taken over by yet another member of the family, Miss Jukes (Marjorie, daughter of 'Miss Hilda').

This was a time of expansion for St Helen's. The original plot had been extended by the purchase of land fronting Carew Road, and there were now two main buildings on site: the original School House, with the additions of the multi-purpose hall and the New School, and Middle House. In addition to the main site there was Ardenlea, home of Little St Helen's, the Field Garden

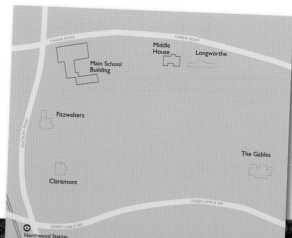

Illustration of the locations of the buildings bought by the school in the 1930s, in relation to the Main School Building and Middle House.

Aerial view of the school, 1935.

The library garden.

across the road, and cottages in Rofant Road. When the original school house was built, it was surrounded by open fields, and more than 30 years later the nearest neighbours were just a few large houses set in big gardens. Within the space of three years, four of these houses suddenly came up for sale. Claremont was the first, in 1934, which briefly became Junior House; in 1935 Longworthe, in Carew Road, beyond Middle House, was acquired as a boarding house; in 1936 first The Gables, in Green Lane, then Fitzwalters, which occupied the space between the main building and Claremont, were also bought.

None of this expansion was planned, although it came at a good time. The school had received favourable publicity in magazine articles in the early 1930s, property was cheap, and the sisters had no real difficulty in arranging loans. With the acquisition of these four properties, the site more than doubled its acreage, and was approaching the size it is today. The large

Garden Room 1932.

'Good Housekeeping' article, 1934.

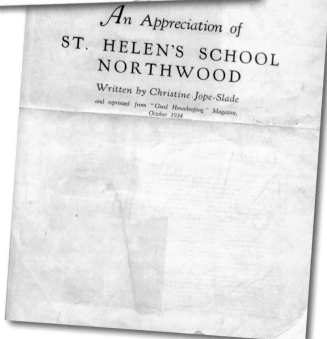

houses were converted for boarding, staff bedrooms, junior girls, and classrooms. Garages and greenhouses found new uses. Fences were pulled down, and the whole area was opened up. There were more tennis courts, gardens, and playing fields.

All was well with the school, and it was evolving steadily. By this time there were about 300 girls, and there was an exceptionally warm atmosphere, especially among the boarders. For the sisters, the pupils were an extension of their own family. The school had a reputation for bringing out the best in any girl, and for producing well-mannered, friendly girls with a sense of duty and service.

But the international situation was looking increasingly grave, and Mrs Broadbent and Mrs Burton-Brown took every

(continued on p. 40)

Opposite: Home Science swimming class, c. 1930.

Swimming

A news cutting of the pool opening, 1930.

The school's first swimming pool opened on 24th May 1930. The steam-heated open-air pool was the first of its kind in the country and attracted much interest from journalists and architects. The pool was quickly put to good use, both during school time and in the summer holidays when it remained open for pupils, friends and relations. Swimming was not, however, always the warmest of sports, as Stephanie Gilbert (Thomson, 1979) recalls: 'We used to watch the ducks swimming on the pool and a few times it actually froze over in winter. Luckily I was a swimmer, but for those that weren't, swimming lessons were probably not much fun. The teachers always used to tell us it was warmer when it was raining but I am not sure how many of us were convinced. The swimmers got to keep warm in the deep end but the non-swimmers shivered as they tried to do widths.'

By the 1970s, the pool was old and cracked so work began to raise funds for a new pool. The school's second swimming pool opened in 1976. Initially open-air, it was covered over in its first year with a retracting roof, which created new challenges for eager, early-morning swimmers, as Stephanie Gilbert remembers, '[On cold mornings] the pool would fog up and you couldn't see from one end to the other and neither could the coach. We all thought it was great fun bluffing the coach as we swam half-lengths because he could not see to the other end. We could see him because he had a lantern round his neck!' Whilst Claire Knust (1994) writes, 'Despite green algae growing on the bottom of the pool … I couldn't be kept out of the water … and swimming at school gave me immense pleasure, achievement and very fond memories.'

Rosie Jackman, current Head of PE, remembers: 'The idea of the roof was great as you could open it in summer and keep it closed in the colder months, but this was not always the case as, as it got older, the roof often jammed open in the cold and refused to open in the heat. My memories of that pool are of the September and October months, being dripped on by the endless condensation and the mist that descended down when it was

Miss Mitchell diving into the new swimming pool, 1930s.

The first swimming pool in use, c.1960.

The second swimming pool in use.

The third swimming pool.

cold outside! In the summer I remember being called regularly to go fishing for frogs or newts who had strayed into the pool. The frogs had to earn their rescue by being used as a teaching aid to demonstrate breaststroke! The death knell for this pool came when the roof began to disintegrate and it had to be closed. It was always quite exciting going to teach swimming, you never knew what was in store.'

Today, the school enjoys the use of its third swimming pool, a modern, 25-metre six-lane indoor pool, built as part of the new sports complex and opened in October 2005 by Olympic bronze medallist, Steve Parry. Debbie Smith (Cook, 1981) writes of this new facility, 'My first memory of sport at St Helen's is of an outdoor freezing swimming pool where we had to change outside. I even remember on occasion having to break a layer of ice before we were allowed to lower ourselves into the icy water ... When I first started teaching at St Helen's, I was amazed to hear about the new swimming pool. What a fantastic facility the girls now have, but whenever I take my Year 2 class past the outdoor pool site I make sure they know what used to be there!'

'I was never very good at sport. In fact, because of my asthma, I was usually given goal positions that didn't involve me having to run around too much. Swimming however, was always a particular hated sport of mine, mainly because I had long hair, and I hated the fact that despite my yellow Bonington coloured swimming cap, my hair always got wet, and it would be dripping down my back all day in a rat-tail ponytail. That and the smell of chlorine that lingered all day in the classroom. For some odd reason, (did I actually want to get in the water in double time?) we always managed to do the 'knicker trick'. That is, put our swimming costume on over our knickers whilst waiting outside to be let into the changing rooms, and managing to then remove our knickers in one swift movement – all under our school dress naturally.'

JOANNA LAWLOR (TWINING, 1994)

Guiding

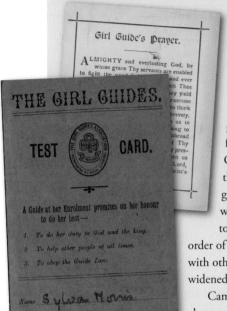

Girl Guide's Prayer.

ALMIGHTY and everlasting God, by whose grace Thy servants are enabled to fight the good fight...

THE GIRL GUIDES.

TEST CARD.

A Guide at her Enrolment promises on her honour to do her best—

1. To do her duty to God and the king.
2. To help other people at all times.
3. To obey the Guide Law.

Name Sylvia Morris

Seaford Guide Camp, 1927.

The Girl Guide Movement was founded in 1910 and Miss Rowland Brown, recognising its benefits as a way of equipping her girls for life at home and in the community, pioneered guiding in Northwood, with the founding of the 1st St Helen's Own company, for boarders, and the 2nd St Helen's Own, for day-girls. Eileen Gibson (Bates, 1915) wrote of the significance of guiding to her, '... to belong to the noble order of the Girl Guides is to link hands with other girls all round the world. It widened our horizons'.

Camp was clearly the highlight of the year, as Fiona Mook-Dewey (Dewey, 1979) recalls: 'the highlights were no doubt the annual summer camp. We set off in the back of a furniture removal van, tents, cooking pots, bags and girls all heaped into the back. On arrival, the first task was to put up the tents, old canvas affairs with two wooden ridge poles, numerous guy ropes and endless wooden pegs that required banging into the hard ground ... We also made the most wonderful contraptions out of bamboo poles and string, including racks to hold the sleeping bags off the ground and washing up stands.

The days were filled with hikes, trails, the inevitable collection of wood for the fire and of course the preparation of dinner using one pan, a spoon and a fire that kept going out. Scrambled eggs with grass never tasted so good. In the evenings, we grouped around the camp-fire and sang traditional guide songs with ridiculous words ... All in all an exciting if exhausting experience.'

During World War Two, the 1st Company moved to Wales whilst the 2nd Company in Northwood grew, resulting in the formation of the new 8th Company, with Miss Dongworth, the school secretary, as Captain. In 1945, when the school reunited, there were three Guide Companies, two Brownie Packs and a Sea

At the Harrow Competition, 1925.

Ranger Crew (introduced in 1944). Guiding continued for many years and the school played an active part in the development of Guiding in Northwood with Mrs Garrett, Miss Edwards and Miss Dongworth all serving as District Commissioners.

The increasing range of extra-curricular activities competed for the girls' attention and its popularity slowly declined. Today, the school still has its own Brownie Pack, one of very few schools to do so.

Opposite: Guides round the campfire.

The riding stables in the late 1930s.

opportunity to hunt out suitable premises for possible evacuation. They also planned underground trenches for the Northwood site, and by early 1939 a long trench was ready, parallel to Green Lane, starting just east of Claremont. It had lights, washing facilities and gas-proof curtains. The accommodation was arranged in bays, so that classes could sit in their own groups and lessons could be carried on.

In the spring of 1939, with war looking inevitable and many schools evacuated to safer areas, Mrs Broadbent took Tregoyd, a large house in Breconshire, Wales, on a seven-year lease, and let the Northwood boarding houses to the Royal Insurance Company. During the summer Tregoyd was fitted out as a boarding school. Practical considerations included organising an adequate supply of safe drinking water, and moving furniture and equipment from

'... the personality of the girls of the school is of such character as is most needed in the world today'.

BOARD OF EDUCATION REPORT, JUNE 1939

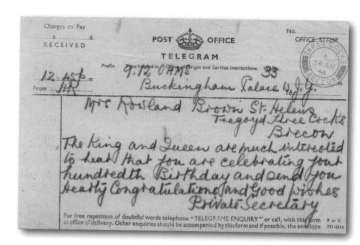

Telegram to Alice Rowland Brown on her 100th birthday, 1944.

> *'During the war we were offered one or two weeks at Llanthomas during the summer holidays ... We had a wonderful time, although Miss Haines was very strict with us! The highlight of our stay was going across the fields to visit Mrs Rowland Brown on her 100th birthday. I remember being chased by geese on the way!'*
>
> MARY ROBINSON (CONNELL, 1953)

Northwood. War was finally declared on 3rd September 1939 and the school divided into two: boarders went to Tregoyd under Mrs Broadbent, day-girls stayed in Northwood under the acting headmistress, Miss Mackenzie. Many of the Northwood parents, faced with the reality of war, now wanted to send their daughters to a safer place away from the bombing. Tregoyd was no longer large enough for everyone so a second house, Llanthomas, was found nearby, and became home to Junior boarders. Despite wartime privations and personal tragic losses, girls at Tregoyd had a quiet war. In beautiful surroundings and held together by team spirit under the Rowland Brown family, they built in Wales a sense of community in exile.

Most of the family were in or near Tregoyd, doing what they could to help – Mrs Rowland Brown (now aged 95) and Mrs Burton-Brown, the Garretts, and Mrs Cavenagh (Ethel), who had been widowed some years before and who would be the first of the sisters to die in 1941. In 1944 Mrs Rowland Brown celebrated her 100th birthday, and received the traditional telegram from the King. She died early the following year, without seeing the end of the war.

The sisters were becoming older, but they found it impossible to retire in the face of the emergency. In a time of shortages and

Leavers' photo, 1926.

difficulties their practical approach to life served them well. Their deep faith and their view of the school as an extended family also helped them to care for those who had suffered loss in the conflict.

The day-girls in Northwood were in the care of Miss Mackenzie – the first time in over 46 years that any part of the school had not been headed by a member of the family. Mrs Jukes ('Miss Hilda') and both her daughters, at different phases of the war, moved in to look after the domestic side of school life. In the Battle of Britain, many hours of lessons took place in the trenches, and sometimes the staff slept there. Throughout the war, as far as petrol rationing allowed, there would be trips between the two halves of the school, exchanging books, news and equipment.

As the end of the war approached, plans were made for the final conversion of St Helen's to a public school. The three 'family' principals all had a financial stake in the school. Mrs Garrett and Mrs Broadbent, both childless, had already expressed their intention of leaving their interests to the school; Mrs Burton-Brown, with a widowed daughter and a grand-daughter to consider, preferred not to do so.

After the war, with the future of the school assured, the sisters finally retired. Mrs Garrett wrote to the Old Girls: 'It has been a wonderful privilege to have been given this work to do, and the life of the school has prospered under God's blessing. I pray Divine guidance will be given to St Helen's throughout its history.'

Within a year or two the surviving sisters had all moved to Milford-on-Sea in Hampshire – May and her husband; Hilda, Beatrice and Doris, all widowed; and their cousin Constance, who had never married. They stayed in close touch with the school and Old Girls, and visited Northwood regularly, as long as their health permitted. Milford was popularly known as 'St Helen's-by-the-Sea'.

'We had morning walks through the country lanes before school in crocodile, after an inspection to see that all boots were properly laced and in order. In ones, twos and threes we were invited at times to tea in the drawing room with the principals. This was shattering in prospect but delightful in retrospect.'
CHARLOTTE DAWSON (HEYWOOD, 1912)

Miss Edwards

Miss Edith Edwards, fondly known by her pupils as 'Teddy' and as 'Eddy' by the staff, joined St Helen's in 1931 as a new Maths graduate. She spent the whole of her working life at the school until she retired in 1968. She quickly became a key figure at the school.

When the school moved to two sites at the outbreak of war, Miss Edwards went to Tregoyd as senior mistress and timetabler. Her sense of humour and pragmatism helped to deal with challenges both at Tregoyd and at Northwood. After returning to Northwood, she became Deputy Headmistress, firstly to Mrs Broadbent, then to Miss MacKenzie and finally to Miss Leader, as well as teaching Maths and managing timetabling.

She juggled several tasks at once whilst retaining a 'quiet calm authority', Janet Chilton (Lindley, 1946). Mrs Sheila Nash said in the 2001 'Old Girls' Magazine', 'It was only when I had become Deputy Head and Head of the Mathematics Department that I fully realised how much Eddy had crammed in, apparently effortlessly, into her working days – teaching, the boarding, the timetables, the organisation of exams, the Arts Competition, Speech Day and so on, and particularly the time to listen to staff and girls. Her dedication to the school was extraordinary, and her genuine interest in all that that involved made her special to those of us who knew her.'

On her retirement in 1968, Miss Leader said of Miss Edwards at Speech Day, 'We do not look forward to being without you; competence and organisational ability can be replaced but loving kindness is an irreplaceable quality'. She had clearly left a lasting impression on all who had had the honour of knowing her during her many years at St Helen's.

Miss Mackenzie and Miss Edwards, c.1949.

Opposite: Tregoyd.

Memories of Wartime – *Bob Ukiah (Resources Director)*

The Library at Tregoyd.

Mrs Broadbent wrote describing how many pupils spent the war years in Wales: 'Those six happy years we spent in that lovely part of Wales were passed in peace and beauty. I never once heard a siren – and they will remain a wonderful memory to many of us, staff and girls.'

Once in Wales, the girls and staff felt safe. Miss Edwards said, 'only once were we in real danger and that was one very stormy night when we were awakened by bangs which we thought might be thunder, but next morning it was discovered that there were 13 small bomb craters in a straight line between Llanthomas and Tregoyd'.

Rosemary McLure (Mardon, 1945), remembers that, 'we all had a very, very happy time down in Wales, plus the excitement of travelling back to Paddington from Hereford at the end of each term. We were equally excited at the start of each term, completely ignoring our mothers while we exchanged holiday news!'

Janet Chilton (Lindley, 1946) was equally positive. 'Potatoes were harvested, firewood gathered, foxglove leaves and rosehips picked, gardening fairly willingly performed and the prefects had the dubious privilege of feeding the hens, in winter by hurricane lamp at 6.30 am.' Rosemary McLure remembers: 'The local farmer wanted his potato field weeded so several of us sixth formers got on our bikes for the two-mile journey to his farm. We did his weeding and as a thank you he gave us all a glass of scrumpy straight off his apple press. It was delicious! On our way home we all felt woozy and had to sit on the grass bank at the side of the lane until we recovered and could ride our bikes without falling off.'

Molly Bradley-Kidd (Robson, 1942) recalls how the girls and staff quickly adapted to life in Wales: 'No electricity, there were acetylene lamps that had to be lit by tapers and, despite wartime rationing we had wonderful food ... Our lacrosse pitch was a field on a slope ... We walked to Glasbury Church every Sunday using a shorter route across a field if Sister Cotterall was on duty or all the way by road if Matron Babington was escorting us as she didn't like the mud or the bull.'

A common recollection is that there was more freedom than in Northwood. Many of the girls had bicycles and became adept at speeding around the countryside. Janet Chilton remembers that, 'when we were bicycling you would get behind terrific convoys of troops, and as each lorry passed they would shout and yell at all us girls bicycling away'.

Elizabeth Grant, Mrs Burton-Brown's granddaughter, who came to Wales in 1942 'after a strange journey with my mother, a young widow, from Geneva ... in a dark plane without air pressure to a bombed-out grey Liverpool and thence to Hereford', recalls, 'Another joy was going riding with Mrs Elwyn-Jones twice a week on little Welsh ponies. She was a farmer's wife, of joyous temperament, who loved taking us through lanes and fields alongside the river Wye. Much of the countryside was abandoned, with neglected orchards, not a soul to be seen. Heels down, knees together, sit up straight!'

Not that life was perfect. Indeed, 'the sausages for breakfast were disgusting. I used to take them out and bury them in the garden' (Janet Chilton). Elizabeth Grant remembers, 'One day we could not eat the sausages, which were always pretty horrid, and for once the grown-ups relented. It turned out that the new boy at the butchers had stuffed the sausages with pepper instead of bread-crumbs. I don't remember lunch except the dreaded fish on Fridays. It was usually off by the time it reached us in mid-Wales and the smell was appalling and made me retch.' Mary Begg (1948) remembers that, 'me and my friends had the most terrible chilblains. We used to vie with who had got the worst chilblains. Bitterly cold. Cold in bed.'

Despite the deprivations (including only being allowed sweets on Sundays and a limit of one bath a week), the girls threw themselves into the war effort. Miss Edwards said, 'I was filled with admiration for the senior girls, for they stayed indoors and sat for hours machining rolls of blackout material to make curtains for the huge windows'. Once that task had been completed, the girls took to knitting. Miss Edwards remembered that 'large sacks of wool used to arrive and everyone knitted for the forces in every spare moment.

In break you could stand knitting with the other end of the scarf wrapped round you,' while during lessons Jean Begg (1945) recalls that 'we mastered the art of knitting with the needles up the sleeves of our blazers so that we could continue undisturbed'.

The war experience for those remaining in Middlesex was different. Northwood was regularly at risk and preparations for attack were comprehensive. Gas masks were issued and trenches were dug. Furthermore, Miss Mackenzie remembered that 'anticipating the Battle of Britain we had watertight huts erected at each of the trenches, and in them were stored mattresses and blankets. When the Battle did come, the staff slept down there.'

The trenches were used daily and Mary Rose Seldon (1947) remembers that 'sometimes we would go down in the morning and not emerge into daylight until the late afternoon. The length of our stay might become tedious, but to the girls the siren itself hardly ever brought displeasure. Down went our pencils and off we trooped, welcoming the break.' Jean Crump (Lermit, 1946) remembers that, 'Towards the end of the war we could spend almost all day in the shelter. I reckon that being near London our siren used to go off whenever London went off as well, and when the planes weren't anywhere near us.'

Caroline Molyneux (Pickup, 1952), remembers the trenches vividly: 'I remember the whole school having to go to the shelter and how the stories of the sixth form students scared me more than the possibility of being bombed or the fright of having to wear our gas masks.'

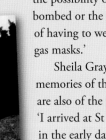

Sheila Gray's (1945) memories of the war are also of the trenches: 'I arrived at St Helen's in the early days of the war. Early memories are of considerable time spent down in the air raid shelter which was a long zig-zag tunnel

The grounds at Tregoyd.

underground … There were slatted benches all along one side where we sat and the staff endeavoured to keep us occupied. I did not envy them their task. Despite these interruptions we did manage to do some academic work.'

Despite the threat, Mary Rose Seldon writes that 'no material damage was done to the school during the blitz'.

School traditions continued, including a concern for the welfare of others, as Miss Mackenzie recalled, 'In the early days of the war ... Mrs Garrett telephoned me one day to say there were many Jewish refugees in the neighbourhood and asked if we could do anything to help. This was typical of her. In consequence we arranged for them to use the Hall every weekend for the Jewish Sabbath and their special Festivals.'

Towards the end of the war, pilotless rockets (V1s and V2s) caused some damage. Miss Mackenzie recalls what could have been a tragedy: '... several girls taking the then Higher Certificate examinations sat for a three-hour paper. The examination ended at 5 p.m. and the girls went home. Twenty minutes later a V2 dropped in Northwood Hills and there was a loud explosion. When I emerged from under the drawing room piano, I went up to the room in which the girls had sat for their examination. It was a shambles. Huge, jagged pieces from the plate glass windows were embedded in the desks and chairs where the girls had been sitting only 20 minutes before.'

Felicity Yuille (West, 1947) evokes the sense of excitement. She says that 'once, I remember, during a Latin lesson in New School we heard a strange noise over towards the railway line: "Oh, look at that strange plane with flames coming from the back", we choroused. It was an early V1.' She goes on to say that 'we used to go round collecting bits of metal out of the holes, where the bombs went off, and keep them. I remember having a shoe-box full of bits of shrapnel from various bombs.'

The School was reunited in Northwood in 1945. In the words of Miss Edwards, 'It was with very mixed feelings that we left Tregoyd in July 1945; it had been a happy time in the life of St Helen's, but we now had to face a new challenge, that of carrying on all the fine traditions of the school in what could be a difficult post-war period'.

Next page: Pageant, c. 1912.

Continuity and Change

Susan Hamlyn

Just as Europe had been divided and fragmented by World War Two, St Helen's had for six years existed as two communities 150 miles apart and run by distinct leadership teams. Its two pupil populations had scant contact over these years. Families had lost loved ones in the conflict, had seen their houses and businesses damaged or destroyed; everyone had a story to tell. During the war, the school buildings in Northwood had been neglected and four of them had been leased to the Royal Insurance Society.

Eight years before her retirement, with characteristic insight, Mrs Broadbent had appointed Miss Ann Mackenzie as senior English mistress. In 1939, when Mrs Broadbent moved the boarders to Tregoyd, Miss Mackenzie, 'Mac', stayed in Northwood as acting head. On Mrs Broadbent's retirement Miss Mackenzie was, despite her youth and relatively short service in the school, the obvious successor but she faced formidable challenges. She wrote, '... the two streams of the school, in Wales and in Northwood, flowed together again as if there had never been a separation' but this considerably understates the task involved. Few heads take up their post at the same time as having to amalgamate two schools and make them run as one. There was duplication in the staff room, day and boarding girls did not know each other and their six years of separation had provided disparate wartime experiences. Miss Mackenzie and Mrs Broadbent had made regular fleeting visits to each other's domains but this was at a time when petrol was rationed and communication difficult. Maps were forbidden in

cars because of wartime restrictions. Alongside the bombing and the privations, pupils were unable to speak to family and friends for months at a time. Northwood girls had German bombs to fear. Tregoyd and Llanthomas girls knew of the bombs but could not know on whom they were falling. Not surprisingly, perhaps, it took time for the two communities to understand each other fully and to recognise each other's different experiences.

Whatever the strains involved in reuniting the two branches of the St Helen's family, no one doubted that the world had changed

Miss Mackenzie in the new library, 1959.

Girls in the library garden, c.1955.

dramatically. The principles of Christian duty and discipline on which the Rowland Browns had founded St Helen's were devoutly shared by Miss Mackenzie but could no longer survive as unquestioned articles of faith. The school buildings needed much work and in post-war Britain money, labour and materials were scarce. The school population had grown and, even with the return of the four houses leased to the RIS, more space was needed but red tape hindered proposed construction work.

Miss Mackenzie's leadership was essential in steering the school back to unity and stability. Having arrived at St Helen's in 1937, she knew what the school and its beautiful grounds had looked like before the war. One of her first appointments was of Miss Hazel Samman as head gardener. Miss Samman remained until her retirement in 1966 and it is to her creativity and labour that the gardens, enjoyed and remembered with affection by so many, owe their existence.

'I can't talk about St Helen's without mentioning the grounds. They were beautiful … Miss Samman used to wear a brown overall with a leather belt at her waist, and she nurtured and loved her gardens. There were herbaceous borders everywhere; delphiniums, peonies, lupins and red hot pokers. There was a field next to Gables. In summer, we lay on our cloaks and read, hidden among the grasses.'

ROSALIND CARRECK (1964)

Mindful of the increased numbers, Miss Mackenzie acquired 'Thirlmere' in 1946 and adapted it to become the new, enlarged Little St Helen's. Fitzwalters ceased to be chiefly a home for staff and was refurbished to provide five classrooms and a laboratory, while still housing a few domestic staff. The next year saw further building and adapting and also a second major staff appointment – that of Dr Dudley Baker as School Medical Officer. The young

(continued on p. 54)

The Parents' Association – *Janet Kirchheimer (Ritchie, 1969)*

Children's BBC presenter Andy Crane opening Fun Day, 1995.

The Parents' Association (now the Parent Teachers Association) has existed since 1951. Originally only open to Junior School parents and used as a vehicle for staff to give talks on educational subjects and to meet parents, the Association was opened to all parents in 1954.

Over the years, the Association has given many gifts which have provided facilities for the girls. In 1967 a pond and fountain were built in the centre of the quadrangle which were enjoyed by generations of girls. Money has been donated to fund Speech Day prizes, building projects and for minibuses and a language laboratory.

While the school had its outdoor swimming pool, the Parents' Association took over running the summer holiday swimming club (with the profits going to the school). When the first pool was built indoors, the swimming club continued to be open daily throughout the summer for the benefit of all members of the school and their families.

Another long-standing service to parents which also raised money for the school is the clothing exchange. When I became involved with the PA in the early 1990s, the clothing exchange was a huge event at the end of the summer term, to which all new parents were invited, with another at the end of the autumn term. Parents would bring their donations to the sale, which would be sorted through and placed on the groaning tables or clothes racks.

The PA also has a long history of running social events from balls, barn dances, tennis tournaments, quizzes, lectures and the most recent addition to the yearly calendar, Fun Day. This started in the early 1990s and is the biggest day in the PA calendar. It is an ambitious undertaking and requires great organisational skills, raising thousands of pounds.

Current Chair of the PTA, Michelle Weerasekera, describes it as 'an important part of the community, made up of parents from all sections of the school. We come together to raise funds through fun social events which still include the very successful clothing exchange, a Secrets Room for junior school children to purchase Christmas presents, a party for Little St Helen's, a highly entertaining quiz night and Fun Day. It gives the people involved a great opportunity to meet other parents and to use their experience to enhance their daughters' education.'

PTA at Calendar Sale, 2008.

School Food

The dining room, c.1910.

The dining room, c.1935.

For many, fond memories of school dinners remain. Amy Calam (1998) writes, 'I still dream about St Helen's lunches to this day. The chocolate pudding and chocolate custard stands out in particular.'

School puddings were a highlight for several others: 'As a junior we all ate in Gables and as a senior you could volunteer to be a server ... I remember jumping at the chance – the cooks at Gables knew how to serve up a chocolate pudding ... This pudding, made in the traditional pudding basin, turned upside down on the plate, would be steaming, and dripping down the sides ... was this most amazing thick white icing. Just superb!', Stephanie Gilbert (Thomson,1979). Whilst Janet Kirchheimer (Ritchie, 1969) remembers, 'lovely rice puddings made in metal roasting dishes came at the end of each lunch ...'

The puddings were even credited with staving off illness, as Gaynor Richardson, assistant matron at Gables in the 1950s, writes: 'I, along with three other pupils out of 49 avoided "Asian flu". We put it down to rice pudding every night for supper!'

And it is not just the girls who were treated to such delights, as Judith Botten recalls: 'I will always remember being brought morning coffee and afternoon tea beautifully laid out on a silver tray and everything was wonderfully genteel!'

However, others do not have such favourable memories of their gastronomic experiences. Rosalind Carreck (1964) remembers: 'Our food was pretty grim by today's standards ... Vegetables were over-cooked, the smell of cabbage wafted around the dining-rooms, and we only saw a salad once a week.
- First horror: spam fritters – when you cut into them, they oozed a river of fat.
- Second horror: boiled hearts – eating them replicated a biology lesson.
- Third horror: boiled butter beans, the skins as dry as paper.

Mince was dire, too, and the porridge was always lumpy.' Although, she concedes, 'The cooks produced excellent fried bread which retained its crunch with tinned tomatoes. Steamed puddings were worthy of Mrs Beeton herself, scrumptious with golden syrup or chocolate sauce, and the apple crumble was a triumph.'

Opposite: The dining room, c.1966.

The dining room, c.1990.

The 1948 Olympics

When it was confirmed that London would be hosting the Olympics there was a great sense of excitement across Britain. Food and accommodation were in short supply in the post-war years. Military barracks were modified for male athletes and boarding schools were made available to the women, amongst them St Helen's.

The star of the Olympic Games was a 30-year-old Dutch housewife and mother, Fanny Blankers-Koen, a member of the Dutch women's team who stayed and trained at St Helen's.

Blankers-Koen was the oldest woman in the Olympic track events. The British team manager dismissed her as being too old to compete. In the Netherlands, critics believed she would be better employed looking after her children. Her detractors might have been even more vocal had they known that she was in the early stages of pregnancy.

She won four gold medals in eight days and it is probable that she would have won six had she not been confined by the rules to competing in three individual events.

Blankers-Koen, who died aged 85 in 2004 having revisited St Helen's in 1988 to make a documentary about the Olympics, was the first mother to win an Olympic medal and the first and only woman to have won four gold athletics medals at a single Olympics, a haul matched in Olympic history by just two other male competitors. In 1999, the governing body of track and field sports, the IAAF, voted her the greatest female athlete of the 20th century.

Fanny Blankers-Koen.

doctor could hardly have anticipated quite how long – and how important – his relationship with St Helen's would turn out to be.

By 1948, the mood had clearly changed from one of recovery and rebuilding the school community to one of celebration. First in a series of happy events was the school's welcome of 140 overseas female competitors in the London Olympic Games. St Helen's accommodated the athletes over the summer. Most famous among them was Dutch athlete Fanny Blankers-Koen who won four gold medals in the Games – a thrill enjoyed by all who shared in the hospitality afforded to the team and by the whole school when it returned in September.

The following year saw the school's best public exam results – a fitting way to mark The St Helen's Golden Jubilee. Remarkably, this occasion was attended by the three surviving Rowland Brown sisters. It was the number of people who celebrated that day which showed that a new school hall was needed. The opening ceremony was disrupted by a storm and everyone crammed into a marquee. The Council of Governors, in view of the exigencies of austerity Britain, proposed a ten-year funding plan which would eventually result in a hall to be dedicated to the founding family. Miss Mackenzie recorded the cheery scepticism of her pupils over whether the hall would ever be built. Ten years is a long time when you are 11.

In 1951 with world tensions high and fears about the possibility of another evacuation, the Governors bought Plas Dinam in Montgomeryshire and opened it as a preparatory school under the guidance of Old Girl, Aileen Cookson, now Mrs Allen. Plas Dinam never accommodated more than 35 pupils but it kept going for four years until fears of conflict receded and most of its pupils joined 'big' St Helen's. Plas Dinam's pupils recalled an idyllic childhood there.

Changes in society were increasingly reflected in the make-up and running of the school. A Parents' Association was founded in 1951 – the Festival of Britain year when a fresh egalitarian spirit was renewing the nation – and grew into a major support for the school, as well as contributing generously to fund-raising activities and prizes. By 1960, Miss Mackenzie reported, somewhat edgily, 'we have now so many silver cups that we do not need more!' This parental involvement coincided with the relaxing of the unwritten law that schoolmistresses were to be single, resident at the school and must inevitably give up their positions on marriage. This liberalisation became, in due

The Chapel – *June Leader*

A small room, full of significance because everything in it was given by people who valued what it stands for. It was often called 'the centre of the school' and when it was created that was the hope – that the spirit of Mrs Garrett's feelings for her school would be endurable and remain potent.

It was never big enough to hold all the boarders on Sunday, yet it was used on Friday evening, and with the help of the extra chairs given as her leaving gift by Miss Edwards when she retired, the Chapel could hold all but the youngest so whatever the week had been there were a few quiet and reflective moments as we said compline.

The altar had been moved from Gwyer, and it was of some historical interest, being made from oaks which came from Moor Park and commissioned by Mrs Garrett. The wood was treated to become light oak rather than its original dark colour. The reredos of the Nativity above the altar was sculpted, and given, by Old Girl, Julian Allan, who owed her training as a sculptress to Mrs Garrett who had supported her when Julian's family could not do so; consequently Julian retained great affection and gratitude to the school which had given her education and life. The gentle young Madonna standing in the niche on the stairs en route to the Chapel was another part of this gift.

Miss Gwyer and Dame Lucy Sutherland gave the pewter cross, candlesticks and vases which furnish the altar, and a small stained glass window, also from Gwyer, was let into the right hand wall, and lighted when Chapel was used. The kneelers before the altar were stitched by various members of staff, who gave their time to this task which I had intended to do for a leaving present, but reality took over and I soon realised it would never be achieved alone and found there were helping fingers who cared to help.

When we had the mercifully rare sadness of death either of staff or pupils, a memorial plaque was put in the Chapel so they were not forgotten in the school to which they had contributed a part of their lives. Similarly the stained glass windows by Joseph Nuttgens based on the line of Vaughn's poetry 'They are all gone into the world of light' was created both as a memorial to Dudley Baker, the school's devoted doctor for 40 years, and as something which would help to beautify this 'quiet place', in the centre of the school.

The Chapel.

'The school to donate the most to Oxfam will meet The Beatles' – *Rebecca Hershman (Baxter, 1964)*

Rebecca Hershman (Baxter) with The Beatles.

This was the tantalising promise made by *The Daily Mail* in the autumn of 1963; an idea masterminded by an, as yet, unknown student affiliated to Brasenose College, called Jeffrey Archer. It would be fair to surmise that, when a portion of the proceeds from Calendar Sale was donated, neither Miss Mackenzie nor the governors appreciated the implications of this action. There was disbelief and astonishment when we won! However, it slowly dawned, to their undisguised relief, that the 'Fab Four' would not actually visit St Helen's and rock the RBH for the adoring 'girls in green'! The girls' disappointment was palpable and there was a sense of being cheated. Instead there would be a 'luncheon' in London at the Westbury Hotel, and Mac with a member of the sixth form would meet not only The Beatles but Mr Harold Macmillan, the Prime Minister. The prize would be an autographed Oxfam poster. The lunch took place but, at the last minute, The Beatles had to cancel. As the chosen recipient of the poster, my disappointment was profound. I was, however, awe-struck by Mr Macmillan, so tall, so charming; he towered over me.

Jeffrey, never known to disappoint, persuaded the Master of Brasenose to hold a *soirée* the following March. Miss Mackenzie would escort me to meet 'The Four' and receive the poster. I had no sense of the complications of such a meeting or the security that proved so necessary. I could tell no one but my parents, who felt bound to provide a second outfit. They too were sworn to secrecy. The time and venue were not confirmed until the afternoon of the actual day, when a note was passed to me in the RBH – '6.30 tonight' – it is my only experience of conspiracy! Mac's driving skills were notorious and we drove to Oxford at a furious pace, my nerves jangling at each sharp bend in the road.

The evening was magical. A small gathering, held in the beautiful private rooms of The Master. Heavy curtains covered the windows and kept us hidden from fans that, later in the evening, started to gather, kept in check by the Oxford Constabulary and necessitating a furtive exit, by a back entrance at the end of the evening. 'Beatle mania' was at its height. Jeffrey Archer, who was at the start of his colourful career, was in his element, steering the proceedings with an intense energy, directing the photographer before requesting that he leave what was, in fact, a private party. Mac charmed and sparkled, enjoying the secrecy as much as I did and rescuing me when nerves overtook me. I had never come face to face with a Liverpudlian and four, all at once, was a real challenge for a sheltered girl from the Home Counties! 'The Four', who were, I suspect, as unsure of their surroundings as I was, were attentive and kind and ensured that we had an amazing evening. I still recall their comments, their individual mannerisms, the food they chose from the magnificent buffet, sitting side by side on the sofa with Paul and George, the shyness of Ringo and the sharp ironic wit of John; their different characters were so clear that evening and a source of constant chatter on the drive home. I forgot to brace myself before each bend in the road.

Mac, who knew little about The Beatles or their music before that evening, took 'prayers' the following morning in her usual calm and dignified way. As the inevitable notices concluded I could feel the stir as everyone waited for the command to dismiss. There was however, a moment's pause, a sudden change of mood, a realisation that our headmistress was enjoying herself. Adjusting her gown and almost casually leaning an elbow on the lectern she delighted in recounting, with a broad grin, our escapade of the previous evening. I doubt that the RBH has ever resounded to such a roar as the girls rose in a wild 'Mexican wave'. That moment was sheer joy. At last I could tell my friends and they could share the thrill.

Plas Dinam.

When I read of Sir Paul playing 'for peace' in Israel or Ringo fronting 'Liverpool as European City of Culture' or when I consider the sad, untimely death of George and the tragic shooting of John, on a New York street, I recall the time St Helen's so nearly met The Beatles!

None of us, in that spring of 1964, appreciated the full significance or possibilities of that poster and it disappeared into a cupboard somewhere. The photographs remain to remind me that, occasionally, something totally unexpected happens, never to be repeated or forgotten; 'a box of delights'!

course, common to all schools but the ethos of St Helen's and its leadership – Miss Rowland Brown had, after all, become Mrs Garrett in 1924 and her sister had become Mrs Broadbent – did not so much allow the community to accede to such changes but, under Mac, positively welcome them.

Husbands of staff were drawn into school life. St Helen's enhanced its 'family' in a warm and innovatory style well before less enlightened establishments. In 1962, Miss Mackenzie in her annual report said that, 'the married staff, of whom there are now many, contribute not only to the academic life of the school, but also to the general interest. Their comments at staff meetings when we are discussing, for instance, the problems of teenagers, are especially valuable when coming from those who have teenage sons and daughters of their own.' Unlike many girls' schools, St Helen's did not try to pretend that boys did not exist. Social events, debates, matches and Summer Balls were regularly held with Aldenham and Merchant Taylors' Schools from the mid-1950s.

Constance Burton-Brown died in 1953. Mrs Garrett wrote, 'her friendly arrival two or three times a week made a great difference to the school, for she was always ready to discuss its many problems and to encourage every effort that was of benefit or added happiness to the school life'. She was the school's first photographer, an entertaining character, creative and selfless. Her contribution remains to this day in the unique photographic

St. Helen's

ROWLAND BROWN HALL APPEAL
1957

Dogs at St Helen's

Miss Leader's Sealyham Terrier, Pippin, is one of, if not the, most memorable pets the school has had. Pippin was walked all over the school by pupils, staff and even interview candidates, and there is a room named after him in Senior School, now the Careers Library. Judith Botten, current PA to the Junior Head, remembers, 'Girls used to call to ask if they could take Pippin out for a walk, which was a lovely way for them to get to know June – and Pippin'.

A portrait of Pippin, now in the library.

Pippin was not, however, the only dog to have featured in school life. Stephanie Gilbert (Thomson, 1979) remembers of her first visit to St Helen's, 'a lovely white dog in the Headmistress's office going by the name of Nimrod' whilst Airedale Terriers could be seen wandering the Bursary Department. Dickon, and later Katie, accompanied Miss Joan Williams, Bursar from 1949 to 1979, to work and Joanna Chaventré (1986) recalls, 'one got used to walking over them when visiting her office'.

record she made and in the hymn and songs she wrote for the school; a 'true comrade and true friend'.

Constance's death added to the pervasive sense of change in the school. School Certificate was being phased out with the introduction of the new GCE O, A and S levels. St Helen's girls, inspired by strong staff, were applying to university in greater numbers. Girls were arriving from Europe and Asia to join a successful sixth form. In the autumn of 1954, Miss Mackenzie appointed a new head of her beloved English department – Miss June Leader, whose service to the school would total 32 years, was just 29 years old. Her mark on St Helen's and on generations of girls she would teach, guide and inspire was to be as profound as that made by any of the dedicated women who had built and shaped the school.

In 1957, after eight hard years of fund-raising, a grand ceremony was held to lay the foundation stone of what would become The Rowland Brown Hall. Above it was to be a splendid new library, lovingly designed by the head of English and to be named after the then Chairman of the Council of Governors, Dame Lucy Sutherland. Fund-raising spanned the entire school community with the girls very much involved. Their contribution was to collect 'A Mile of Sixpences'. Representatives from Junior School and Little Saints were sent to add their contributions, usually resulting from fund-raising activities, but also personal sacrifices of pocket money. Bulletins were issued about the

Miss June Leader with Nimrod.

Opposite: A biology lesson, c.1960.

Music – *Robert Crowley (Director of Music)*

Students in 1911: Eva Seldon (Morley) is pictured far left.

Music has always played a part in the life of St Helen's, mainly restricted in early years to piano and singing, with a few violinists and cellists. From 1916, Mrs Eva Seldon, a former pupil, and Miss Muriel Davidson played a huge part in the development of music as an intrinsic part of school life, as Christine Harris (Fyson, 1926) recalled: 'Almost all my recollections … have a background of varying sounds of music; for there always seemed to be someone playing a piano somewhere. Outside on the swing under the elms, or on the playing field, one heard the constant tinkle through the open windows.'

Miss Davidson would remain at the school for 36 years and Miss Mackenzie attributed the development of the school orchestra, as well as its junior equivalent, to her determination to build up the music department and the inspiration she gave to her pupils.

The music department in Fitzwalters and, since 1990, in Mackenzie, have facilitated many developments in music teaching, offering girls opportunities that remain with them long after leaving, as Jessica Sims (Plumridge, 1996) writes: 'The greatest opportunity my music teacher, Mrs Curtis, gave me was the chance to sing the soprano soloist's part in Mozart's Requiem in the joint St Helen's/Merchant Taylors' concert. I was terrified. But Mrs C, as she was fondly known by many of us, remained firm that I could do it and after some intensive lessons, I performed the piece and still remember it as one of the highlights of my life at St Helen's. I am sure that without the support, knowledge and kindness I enjoyed at school, I would not have gone on to be in the theatre and opera industry as a professional.'

Each year the combined orchestras and choirs of St Helen's and Merchant Taylors' together with the Choral Society, made up of parents and members of staff from both schools as well as former pupils, parents and friends, continue to give a concert.

Since 2006 even the youngest pupils have enjoyed participating in the music carousel when they spend a term discovering the

A concert in the school hall, c.1956.

A music lesson, c.2008.

*The St Helen's/Merchant Taylors'
Joint Concert in the Merchant
Taylors' Great Hall, c.2008.*

keyboard, violin and cello. Once in Junior School individual music lessons are taught by a large number of part-time music staff in instruments as varied as the bassoon, viola and French horn. The Junior School's space in Mackenzie allows groups to discover singing and playing together whilst Fitzwalters' technology suite introduces students to composing, supported by the latest computer software. The PTA's generous gift of £20,000 in 2008 enabled the purchase of new instruments which has helped tremendously with the rapid expansion and development of the concert and jazz bands.

Countless ensembles and groups of varying sizes provide opportunities for girls to perfect their playing. The Junior and Senior Schools boast successful concert and jazz bands, orchestras and choirs. Recent local performance venues include the RBH, and Holy Trinity and Emmanuel Churches in Northwood. In May 2009, the St Helen's Singers sang Evensong at Southwark Cathedral. Regular Senior School music tours take place, most recently to Spain and the Netherlands. Music continues to grow in its variety and popularity and will undoubtedly offer the girls exciting opportunities in years to come.

Mrs Garrett and Miss Mackenzie at the Rowland Brown Hall stone laying ceremony, 22nd June 1957.

progress of the 'Mile' alongside exhortations to remind everyone of how much was still needed. There was huge satisfaction when the 'Mile' was completed and each girl felt a sense of pride in her contribution.

Mrs Garrett performed the stone-laying ceremony before the entire school which assembled on the bottom lax pitch. Although it was 58 years since the school's inception, Mrs Garrett was accompanied on the platform by all the school's headmistresses, past and present, from Northwood and from the years in Wales. There were also three heads of departments, all of whom had served the school for 25 years or more, as well as one of the school's first pupils. Two years later, during the school's Diamond Jubilee, the new hall was opened by HRH The Duchess of

'When I came to St Helen's in 1954 my art room had large church-like windows at each end. We were high up, so when the Rowland Brown Hall was built we had an excellent view. The builders soon discovered they had a fascinated young audience. I set up chairs and drawing-boards so that the children could draw the scene. The builders gave a splendid performance, especially in their break-time, when they sat astride the joists, perhaps 60 feet up or more, drinking out of metal mugs.'

BERYL TAYLOR (HEAD OF ART, 1954–1984)

Gloucester. Once again, all the principals attended this event. Janet Hilken (Sewell, 1971) recalls, 'my friend Rachel Pyper and I were in the kindergarten at LSH. We were the smallest girls in the school. One of us was to be chosen to give the bouquet to The Duchess of Gloucester. Although I was the youngest, Rachel was slightly shorter than I was and she won!' Miss Mackenzie recounted how, 'Mrs Garrett, although in a wheelchair because of arthritis, insisted on seeing *all* the new building. Our faithful gardeners and house staff carried her right to the top where she saw the splendid new library and, on the way down, the beautiful little chapel with the altar sculpture.' The new hall accommodated the whole school and the opening ceremony was relayed to the parents who picnicked outside on the lawns. Few schools could boast so strong a sense of family, continuity and dedication as St Helen's experienced that day. That same year, two members of staff, Miss Fox and Miss Pearson, retired. Between them they had given 54 years of service to the school.

The new building made a great difference to the life of the school and remains as a monument to the inspiration of its creators. Miss Mackenzie oversaw the project over ten arduous years and she paid tribute to her colleagues, and to the wider school community, especially to 'the wise guidance' given by the Governors and Dame Lucy, the 'generosity of pupils (past and present) and of parents and friends, and, above all, to the

The official opening of the Rowland Brown Hall by HRH the Duchess of Gloucester, July 1959.

Opposite: Girls at the opening of the RBH, July 1959.

Miss June Leader with girls in the new library, 1959.

A trip to Coventry Cathedral.

optimism and unfailing efforts of the staff'. The new library, as all who have worked in it will testify, was a valuable addition. Reminiscent of the reading room in an old college, the library generated an atmosphere of quiet, pleasurable scholarship. Miss Leader, its visionary designer, set about stocking it with a store of books. The quiet beauty of the chapel, the lofty and elegant proportions of the hall and the newly-released space elsewhere considerably enhanced the school.

While extra-curricular activities had long been lively at St Helen's with the diary in the 1940s full of outings, entertainments and outside speakers, clubs and societies flourished as never before. The school diary for the 1950s illustrates the cultural wealth available at the school. Girls attended concerts given by maestri such as Nina Milkina, Ernest Reed and Robert Mayer, operas at Sadler's Wells, lectures by luminaries such as Sir John Hunt, Sir Edmund Hillary, C V Wedgwood and went to plays in Stratford-on-Avon and London to see the theatrical greats of the era from Margaret Wolfit to Laurence Olivier.

Inside the school, once the new hall and library had become assimilated into daily life, there was more expansion over the next few years. Buildings were extended – the dining room on a regular basis. New subjects, such as Spanish and dancing, found

permanent places in the curriculum and sporting prowess was encouraged. Tennis was especially successful and, one year, the first team made it to the final of the Aberdare Cup. Miss Mackenzie undertook to drive the girls – with Miss Edwards in her car following with the remainder of the team – to the great match which took place on a very stormy day. A branch crashed down on Mac's car, terrifying everyone in both cars, and the girls did not play their best in the matches that followed. 'I think they might have won,' reflected Miss Mackenzie, 'if the weather had not been so dramatic'.

It was, perhaps, the arts which made most progress in these years. Music flourished for more than 40 years under the much-loved Miss Muriel Davidson, and later, briefly, under Mrs Ross. By the early 1960s the school boasted several orchestras, choirs

> 'A most valuable resource was the library and reasonable requests to the librarian, Roseen Freeth, were usually acquired ... Our collection in the library was compared favourably with various colleges where students were less well provided for.'
>
> VALERY COWLEY (ENGLISH DEPARTMENT, 1969–1989)

and ensembles. Art classes, under Miss Taylor and encouraged by a large, new studio, produced varied and stimulating work. The art and music departments collaborated with the ever-inventive Miss Leader to produce school plays which have become legendary. The Leader-Ross collaboration even resulted in a decision to stage the first St Helen's 'musical' the work chosen being 'Iolanthe'. Miss Mackenzie also recalled 'remarkable' productions of, in particular, Miss Leader's beloved Shakespeare but also of 'Murder in the Cathedral', Gilbert and Sullivan and 'The Beggar's Opera'. Many former pupils remember the excitement of taking part whether musically, artistically, technically or dramatically in these productions. Judith Weedon (Pickup, 1956) recalled 'the excitement and fun, as a junior, of being chosen to be one of the fairies in the senior school production of "A Midsummer Night's Dream" and learning the unforgettable but only words, "And I!"'.

Academically, St Helen's was making rapid progress. In 1962, Miss Mackenzie reported that 37 girls had entered for A levels, 81 for O levels and that the number of girls taking arts and sciences was more or less equal. She also reported that, for the first time, five girls had taken O levels in cookery and in dressmaking. Results were encouraging. Four girls passed needlework and all five passed cookery. The following year 17 and 19 girls respectively sat exams in these subjects. By 1966,

Fire Dance at the Pageant of London, 1973.

Duke of Edinburgh

'"D of E is not a competition but we won it anyway" is what comes to mind when I remember all the times we had to sleep in every layer we had brought or climb hills which were unimaginably steep. However, when we got back on the coach after we had finished our ventures into the countryside, there was a buzz of hyperactivity and relief that we had survived walking along the edges of cliffs and would soon be home to enjoy a long bath. The jokes cracked and the fun had on those few expedition days is enough to overcome the falling in cow pats and sleep not had, and given the choice, I would do it all over again.' (Laura Wilson, current pupil)

A sentiment that is doubtless shared by the many girls who have completed their Bronze, Silver or Gold Duke of Edinburgh's Awards at St Helen's. Since its introduction in the 1960s, D of E has become an increasingly popular activity at the school with nearly half of Year 10 and 11 participating and an impressive number pursuing Gold Awards in the Sixth Form. The combination of undertaking an expedition, to places such as the Isle of Wight and the Peak District, the development of personal interests, physical activity and service to others has proved enduringly attractive to the girls.

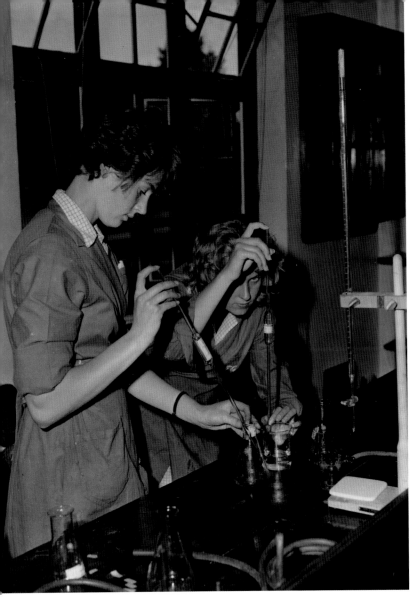

Science lesson, c. 1960.

acknowledged by the women's liberationists whose mothers and grandmothers had been its first beneficiaries. In 1963, St Helen's celebrated Mrs Garrett's 90th birthday. Mrs Garrett herself was too frail to visit the school so the school went to her. She held a lunch and tea for a few of her oldest Old Girls. Miss Edwards surprised the company with a tape of a special school assembly held in her honour on the previous day which included LSH singing 'All Things Bright and Beautiful'. Mrs Garrett was delighted. The following year saw the death of Mrs Burton-Brown at 85 and Mrs Garrett herself died in 1965 at 91 years of age. The school she had started in 1899 with 12 girls had grown to a community of 600.

With the passing of the 1960s came the passing of an entire era. In January 1971, the last remaining Rowland Brown sister, and the longest-serving of the school's headmistresses until then, Mrs Broadbent, died at the age of 90. Her devotion to school and girls was unquestioned even if her approach had been somewhat uneven, as described in 'The First Eighty Years': 'She never gave up a difficult child; some felt that she tried too hard to help them and "she could be extremely uncomplimentary" but most are eternally grateful to her and to that little half smile so full of compassion and understanding with which she dismissed them after a serious talk. She loved all her children, it must be confessed, some more than others but her favourites were not necessarily the most able or the best behaved, such was her sympathy for childish high spirits ... her greatest care was for the unsung multitude or average ability or less'. In 1961, the long-serving school cleaner had retired. That he was always known only by his surname also marks a change. Miss Mackenzie wrote, 'another faithful servant of the school, Hinson, retired last October after 38 years at St Helen's. How patient he has been with thoughtless school girls who have brought in mud after he had just polished floors and stairs.'

'My mother and I spent the late summer and early autumn of 1957 visiting girls' boarding schools across the south-east of England ... St Helen's was different. Instead of the terror of a formal interview, we were invited to tea with Miss Mackenzie in her drawing-room. She had a beautiful low voice and tremendous presence, but she was not intimidating.'

ROSALIND CARRECK (1964)

on Miss Mackenzie's retirement, 20 girls were taking A levels in three science subjects, nine Old Girls had places at art schools, and three candidates for Oxbridge all gained places. More than a third of the sixth form was now applying to university. By 1970, the headmistress was able to report strings of A grades at both O and A levels in everything from maths to A level needlework. St Helen's was making a significant showing in the ranks of academic schools.

The 1960s were a time of change and of leave-taking. Girls' education, a new and radical project in late Victorian times, was, of course, taken for granted by the 1960s. The struggles and dedication which had brought it into being were not always

Ten Tors – *Rosie Jackman (Head of PE)*

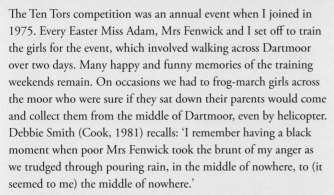

The Ten Tors competition was an annual event when I joined in 1975. Every Easter Miss Adam, Mrs Fenwick and I set off to train the girls for the event, which involved walking across Dartmoor over two days. Many happy and funny memories of the training weekends remain. On occasions we had to frog-march girls across the moor who were sure if they sat down their parents would come and collect them from the middle of Dartmoor, even by helicopter. Debbie Smith (Cook, 1981) recalls: 'I remember having a black moment when poor Mrs Fenwick took the brunt of my anger as we trudged through pouring rain, in the middle of nowhere, to (it seemed to me) the middle of nowhere.'

On the whole the girls really made the most of the experience which was at times hard, but extremely rewarding, and they certainly learnt a lot about themselves and about being outside their comfort zone. For the staff the training was really illuminating and you certainly saw the girls in a different light. Mrs Pat Fenwick, a member of the PE department from 1969 to 1999, recalls 'the unforgettable sight of 2,500 young people leaving at dawn for this

tough expedition'. On the return journey the girls' emotions were like yoyos, high as kites if they had finished, devastated if they had not, but all equally exhausted.

It was a sad day when our entries were no longer accepted due to being outside the designated areas. The last team completed Ten Tors in 1998 and we then had to look at different ways to give the girls an experience to replace it. For two years we took trips to Morocco to climb Mount Toubkal. This proved to be a real-life experience of not only arduous physical exertion but also of being exposed to a very different culture.

Art – *Frances Ames (History of Art teacher)*

The Art Room, early 1960s (now the Sixth Form Common Room).

As the school expanded, so did the Art Department, both in terms of its facilities and its variety of work. In the 1960s, a pottery kiln was installed as part of the new art studio and pottery became a popular option. Beryl Taylor, Head of Art from 1954 to 1984, recalls: 'Once the girls learned the basis, there was no stopping them, and in the Speech Day Display there was always a table with a collection of often primitive, but precious pots, all good enough to encourage further experiments. Pottery became so popular that we started an after-school Pottery Club. Some of the staff wanted to join too, so we had a mixture of girls and staff, which was most successful, and had a social as well as a constructive value. We had a great deal of fun, and the standard of the pottery improved fast. Eventually it became necessary to employ a professional potter to instruct the older girls, as they were out-growing my capabilities!'

Art lesson with Miss Beryl Taylor.

Pottery with Miss Beryl Taylor, c.1959.

A Senior art lesson.

to resources has been interactive white boards, where any painting can be displayed within a few seconds and virtual tours can be taken of the architecture being studied.

The school's proximity to London and its many excellent galleries has always been a bonus for the girls and today the Musée d'Orsay in Paris can also be reached for a day's drawing, whilst art historians make trips to galleries as far away as Washington, DC and New York.

In 1981 the Art Department moved to the new June Leader building where it has thrived. The Art Department in 2009 is committed to the very traditional artistic pursuit of drawing from observing the human form and in the sixth form life-drawing is a weekly discipline. Digital photography and computer-aided design are also important and widely used tools as a significant, up-to-date form of artistic expression. Art flourishes at GCSE, AS, A Level and as part of the International Baccalaureate. A highlight at the end of each academic year is the exhibition of a wide range of exciting work in the June Leader building.

History of Art developed from Mrs Garrett's weekly Art Talks, which were innovative at a time when universities did not recognise History of Art as a serious subject, to being taught as a component of A Level, to a full AS and A Level, where pupils study the development of the history of Western Art. An important addition

Sixth Form art, c.2001.

Old Girls' Club – *Mary Rose Seldon (1947)*

Old Girls' Group.

This book intends to explain the 'family feeling' which has always existed at St Helen's. For Old Girls, the school is far bigger than in their time but the 'family feeling' remains and has even been commented on by school inspectors. At the 110th milestone many Old Girls cherish personal memories of The Family who founded this school.

By 1903 Old Girls were being asked for news of their progress. All of the first 12 pupils maintained their connection throughout their lives. The school and OG Club shared the annual magazine until 1959. In the 1919 edition there are accounts of special events and reminiscences of school life. In 1929 an editor was appointed and the magazine included material on the Library, Calendar Sale, a list of Births, Deaths and Marriages and letters which today would appear under 'People and Places'. Old Girls were already travelling the world, and writing back to school to share their experiences.

The Old Girls' Weekend soon became popular. There was a cricket match, a dance, and boarders had to move out as Old Girls delighted in sleeping in the dormitories! The Old Girls' gathering has always been on a weekend near to the Founder's birthday. The long tradition of greeting that day by surprising Mrs Garrett with bunches of flowers held high has given way to a new tradition as OGs thank senior leaving staff with big pots of daisies.

Elsewhere you will read of the school's tradition of Calendar Sale, very much part of any St Helen's girl's life. Deaconess Murch's Mission in Hoxton, and later The Settlement in Islington, depended greatly on the school's contributions, and Mrs Broadbent always ran a stall at Calendar Sale for The Settlement. The Calendar Sale features in every OG magazine; chosen charities show interests and concerns fostered when at school. A cot for a child in hospital was an early favourite, and May Haythornthwaite (1917), who founded a leper clinic in India, was a name known by generations. Recently the Club has helped children in Zambia and Brownies in Romania as well as many appeals nearer home. For years we supported an OG doctor working in Pakistan near the Afghan border. Earlier we helped an OG who translated the Bible into Urdu. Gap Year adventures are also on today's list.

In the 1930 OG section of 'St Helen's Own' we read: 'Old Girls turned up [to Calendar Sale] in great force ... one was heard plaintively to say "But the only thing I *really* like is the bag I brought" – "Well , *buy it back*" was the stern reply ... and she did.' Many aspects of the school have changed but every OG can still recognise something of herself at St Helen's.

Miss Mackenzie guided the Northwood School through the War and eventually in 1946 there was an OG Day again, the Family present and a number of OGs in uniform. Only one wartime edition

Mrs Mary Webster and staff at Old Girls' Day upon her retirement, 1995.

Fifty Years on – Old Girls' Reunion.

Old Girls' Centenary Reunion at Glaziers Hall, 7th May 1999.

of OG news was published with the sections arranged by occupations rather than years – WRNS and ATS, Nurses and Land Girls.

Every OG News today starts with letters from our Headmistresses, Secretary, Treasurer and Editor. The first secretary was Doreen Dowdy, followed in 1930 by Violet Slade Jones, a long-standing supporter of St Helen's. She was succeeded by Christine Harris (Fyson) and during the war Eva Seldon (Morley) began a long period as Secretary. She and Miss Edwards as Treasurer had both worked with the Family and knew many Branch Secretaries personally. These valiant souls feature from the very first edition of the magazine and are as indispensable today, forming the Committee of the Club

After the war, dinners celebrating anniversaries were held in London, often at a hotel. Glaziers Hall was the venue for Miss Leader's retirement dinner and the first event of the Centenary. With Memorial Services for Mrs Garrett and Mrs Broadbent a reconnection with St Helen's, Bishopsgate was forged and an annual service for present school and OGs held, although, with changes in the times, these are no more.

Centenary celebrations filled a sparkling weekend organised by Sally Fleming (Pollott). Mary Rose Seldon handed over her tenure as Secretary to Sally after this jamboree. 'The First 80 Years' was published while it was possible to have many personal memories of that period; this publication, 30 years on, continues the story. Old

Girls thank Mrs Morris and Sally for all they do to keep the link between OGs and the present school alive.

In 1938, as the school became 31 years old, Paule de Lepervanche (Lepestre) recalls OG celebrations, her last sentence as true today as it was then: 'There were those who have remained unaltered through all the changes: it is they who make the spirit of St Helen's something much greater than can be shown by the outward forms of bricks and mortar and who have set a fine tradition which OGs feel so strongly when they come back to St Helen's.'

Mary Rose Seldon and Sally Fleming at the Old Girls' Anniversary Dinner, 1999.

Girls in the quad, 1960s.

"'Forty Years on, as we think of times olden,
Mem'ry will picture our girlhood's bright years,
Forty years on in the dim distance golden
Laughter still ringing, forgotten the tears!"

Actually it's 45 years on for the Class of '64, but this Spot Supper
song is correct – it is the laughter and the friendship we remember,
not the tears. As we all circled the quad on our last day together,
just before our last goodbyes, we sang "We Shall Overcome" in a
spirit so optimistic for the future, but touched with sadness for what
we were leaving behind. It was our St Helen's we took away with
us, and our St Helen's lives on in our memories, just as it does for
every generation.'

ROSALIND CARRECK (1964)

After 29 years at the school, Miss Mackenzie herself retired. In her last annual report she paid tribute to staff, governors and friends while actually naming only a few individuals. The first of the few was Dr Dudley Baker, the School Medical Officer and her personal doctor for nearly 20 years. 'It is thanks to him that I stand before you in such good health today,' she said. Miss Mackenzie's name was commemorated with the purchase of 3 Carew Road as a sixth form boarding house and flat for Miss Leader who was appointed her successor. Mac had made a profound impression on the school, on those who worked under her and on her girls. June Leader recalled her personal generosity and her 'affection mingled with awe' for 'The Family' and how she never allowed the school to forget the traditions they had established. Rebecca Hershman (Baxter, 1964) recalled her 'phenomenal memory', her 'strong Christian principles', the atmosphere of 'busy activity and learning' rather than 'cosiness' she inspired and times when 'her sternness and disapproval could be quite frightening'. But there was another side. Rebecca Hershman recalls a somewhat unlikely event she, as head girl, shared with Miss Mackenzie in 1964, the result of the school winning a competition by raising money for Oxfam (see box on p. 56).

In their appointment of Miss Leader as successor to Miss Mackenzie, the second time in succession that a serving head of English had been given the post, the Council of Governors paid the departing head the greatest compliment. They had, in Miss Leader, fortuitously found a headmistress uniquely qualified to understand, sustain and nurture the school Miss Mackenzie had built – a humane, disciplined and exciting place in which to learn. Remarkably, Miss Leader was only the fourth headmistress in the school's 67-year history and, like Miss Mackenzie, had spent several years at the heart of the school before assuming her headship. Thus, continuity and an understanding of the school's essence were integral to the approach of all four heads to date and perhaps account for the school's special sense of itself, alongside the inestimable benefit it derived from the strong characters of each individual incumbent.

If anyone had thought that the opening of the RBH was to complete the building programme, they were mistaken. Miss Leader – who came to be known as 'Bricks' or 'June the Builder' – inherited her predecessor's drive to meet the needs of her expanding school and added to it her own determination to do it beautifully. When she became head, the school had 560 pupils. By its 80th birthday, 13 years later, there were 830. The building work continued unabated. First came the completion, in 1968, after many years planning, un-planning and re-planning, of the quad. In the following year, Dame Lucy found herself laying yet another foundation stone – this time for a new science block. To mark the advent of the new decimal currency a 'time capsule'

A school trip with Mrs Whittick, 1960s.

was buried behind it, containing sets of both the old and the new currency. Also interred was a panoramic picture of the school, a Churchill crown and copies of *The Times* and of the school magazine. In the following year the new block was opened by Professor Dorothy Hodgkin, the distinguished Nobel laureate. Science was given a boost by the new facilities and within a few years almost as many girls were choosing to pursue sciences as arts.

Miss Leader's aim was not, however, to serve only an academic purpose. True to the original spirit of the school, she sought to 'lead forth' whatever could be found in each girl. 'The

Professor Dorothy Hodgkin opens the new science block, September 1970.

'Mrs Whittick was legendary as an extremely scary senior school teacher when I was in Junior School in 1962. On our forays over to Senior School to use the gym, we used to sneak past Fitzwalters (where the biology labs were) for fear that she'd come out and throw chalk at us, as she was rumoured to do to inattentive pupils in her lessons. It took a while of getting to know her in later years to realise that her apparently fierce nature came from a deep and genuine concern for her students, as well as a refusal to truck with any nonsense from them.

Mrs Whittick's exceptional skill in teaching was her ability to convey what things really* mean, *to get students to see beneath the potentially intimidating scientific jargon to understand the material. I remember she was teaching us how nerve action potentials worked: a chalk line was drawn on the floor to represent the cell membrane, we lined up as potassium or sodium ions on either side, and when she blew a whistle we exchanged sides.

Mrs Whittick was also a very useful person to have around at the time of the exams, as I am sure she was psychic. For both my O and A Levels she double-guessed some extremely difficult questions on the exams and gave them to us in the mocks ...

As a child I was animal mad, and always keen on biology, but Mrs Whittick's contribution to my career was to foster my love for, and understanding of, academic biology ... Mrs Whittick is amused that my current career, as an evolutionary palaeobiologist who uses anatomy to understand the behaviour of extinct mammals, relies on subjects that were barely covered in the biology curriculum: behaviour and evolution.

I see her influence on me continually now through my own teaching. The popular notion exists that middle-aged women will hear themselves say something and exclaim "Oh no, I'm turning into my mother!" For me, I hear words come out of my mouth to my students (at Brown University), and realise that I've turned into Mrs Whittick, especially when I absolutely refuse to patronise them, and hold them to high standards (a difficult venture in these days of political correctness and easy A grades). And while I don't throw chalk at students who chat during my lectures, I have been known to use a water pistol!'*

CHRISTINE JANIS (1969)

June Leader – *Joanna Chaventré (1986)*

June Leader in the new Kennedy building, 1985.

The happy environment that Miss Leader created could not have happened without her dedication to and love of the school. She made St Helen's 'home' for so many girls under her care. Her greatest interest was in the fortunes of the school and she derived tremendous pleasure from its success. Many viewed her as the perfect role model of what a teacher should be, and she believed passionately that teaching was, and is, a valuable and fulfilling profession.

Always immaculately turned out, Miss Leader commanded respect. She made it her business to know everyone by name; one of the many skills mentioned by Natasha Rodikis Presvytis (1986), 'She knew the names of each and every one of us and instilled many values into us, from always being polite and accepting people from all walks of life to always offering to those in need; and that a smile costs nothing.'

If someone didn't come to Calendar Sale, Miss Leader would know. Her presence around school was felt by everyone. It still is when she visits – I find myself sitting up straight or growing an inch taller whenever she enters a room. Her quiet and calm voice was heard by everyone. In assemblies in the Rowland Brown Hall, Miss Leader would walk in the door and instant silence would fall before she walked up the stairs to the stage. She was precise with a great eye for detail and her command of the English language was second to none; even now I do not and never will use the word 'nice'.

Miss Leader always made time to listen to girls, staff and parents. She wanted to know what was going on at every level of the school and to get to know the interests of the pupils and staff. Now, on her many visits to the school, her memory and knowledge or 'her' staff and pupils never ceases to amaze me.

Sue Lister (Maddocks, 1973) recounts how Miss Leader shaped the course of her life: 'In the spring of 1972 Miss Leader suggested to my parents that I might benefit from the experience of taking an art history course at the British Institute of Florence during the Easter vacation. Aged 17 I lacked direction with no clear idea of career plans beyond wanting to do something "arty" and therefore June Leader's legendary perspicacity and sensitivity was to lead directly to what would be a fulfilling career as an art historian and academic administrator in Florence where I have lived for over 30 years. I still have the carefully considered letter she wrote to my parents – I think it should be framed!'

Miss Leader lived, worked and breathed St Helen's. Her final Head's report sums it up beautifully: 'To watch them grow up and to have a small part in their development, is a great privilege: it has been my good fortune to do this, and to teach a – dare I say, the supreme subject, and I am thankful for the life in this school.'

The June Leader Building.

Gymnastics in the new Gymnasium, opened 1976.

Gymnastics, 1970s.

staff and I are concerned to find the right training for the less academic girl,' she wrote. For these girls there were, 'plenty of interesting careers'. She reported, in 1970, that 18 girls had gone to university, seven to training colleges or colleges of music, two were studying domestic science, eight were at secretarial colleges, six to nursing, one to physiotherapy, one to speech therapy, and one to cartography. But those for whom only one or two academic qualifications were a realistic aim were always equally encouraged to find their niche and develop their potential. In this aim they were vastly assisted by the extra-curricular life of the school. Janet Hilken (Sewell, 1971) writes, 'I lived for all the extra-curricular things. I wasn't very academic but I loved getting involved. Calendar sale, Darby and Joan day, games teams, ballet lessons, school plays, orchestra and choir ... We had such fun. It was my school days that made me go on to be a teacher and I am still involved in education today.' Miss Leader's annual reports celebrated especially those pioneering and altruistic Old Girls who, in the days before organised gap year schemes, served in difficult places at home or abroad, often enduring considerable privations and stresses.

The new science block had released space elsewhere, in particular for the music department, now relocated to Fitzwalters. It was graced by the grand piano left to the school by Muriel Davidson, along with her bust of Mozart, both in the new small concert room named after her. However, the attention of 'Bricks Leader' was now needed urgently elsewhere. The swimming pool was dilapidated, cracked and unusable. Far from suffering from fund-raising fatigue, girls, parents and staff laboured as never before – a new swimming pool having, possibly, more appeal than a science block. For the first time, the proceeds of Calendar Sale were divided between the school's charities and the pool appeal, a development with which Miss Leader was, for some time, uneasy. The matter was put to the vote and the decision taken in truly democratic St Helen's style. After dilemmas, distractions and delays, the splendid new pool was opened along with a new gym and squash court in 1976.

The school's growth required a fourth house, Bonington, to be created. Four pre-fabricated classrooms were constructed and the school's original hall was transformed into classrooms as well. In 1977, after years of negotiation, St Helen's bought the

'A Midsummer Night's Dream', July 1985.

former St Philomena's School which abutted LSH and knocked it down, increasing the overall size of the school to 23 acres, a rare amount of space for a London girls' school. It provided for a time a new asphalt area with a tennis wall and general play space. Despite the rapid pace of school construction, the school diaries for these years are full of expeditions, the Duke of Edinburgh's Award Scheme in which the school was an early enthusiastic participant, sports fixtures, musical events, tours and trips, dramatic productions, careers talks and visits, lectures, theatre trips and charity activities.

In 1977 Dame Lucy Sutherland retired after 31 years service on the Council of Governors, 25 of these as chairman. Miss Leader paid tribute to Dame Lucy saying, 'by those of us who belong to her era, Dame Lucy is held in the same affectionate regard, mingled with awe, as Old Girls accord to "The Family". No school in the kingdom has been better, more carefully, served than we have by Dame Lucy ...'. She was succeeded as Chairman by Lady Habakkuk. Two years later, Miss Williams, who had served for 30 years as bursar and *costumière extraordinaire* retired. The school's 80th birthday that year was marked by the publication of 'St Helen's: The First Eighty Years', edited by Old Girl, Rosalind Onians. This book assembled reminiscences and

memorabilia from school archives and from its oldest surviving members and provides an invaluable and readable account of the genesis and growth of the school.

In 1981, Miss Leader announced her engagement to be married to Dr Dudley Baker who had been, by that time, the school's doctor for 35 years. The general amazement was exceeded only by the warmth and delight which greeted this revelation. This was manifest in the decoying of the happy couple into the quad on July 9th where they were presented with the school's wedding present. The marriage took place two days later at St Mary's Church, Harefield. Two months later, the June Leader Building for arts and domestic science was opened – an appropriate memorial to 27 years service to the school and to the fostering of a love both of the arts and of practical skills in the girls.

In 1982, Mrs Eva Seldon, née Morley, died at the age of 87. She had joined the school as a 12-year-old pupil in 1906 and had never severed her links. She joined the staff, having gained her LRAM, in 1916, as a music teacher. On her marriage, she involved her husband in school life and he contributed valuable financial advice to the Council of Governors. Their daughter, Mary Rose, became a pupil, in due course, and, eventually, head girl. Mrs Seldon had contributed invaluably to 'The First Eighty Years' and,

Opposite: 'A Midsummer Night's Dream', 1974.

The Habakkuk Library.

Junior School girls in the Habakkuk Library, 2009.

in 1953, she was appointed secretary of the Old Girls' Club. Miss Mackenzie wrote that she 'became a close personal friend ... and apart from the Rowland Brown family, I can think of no one who has served the school with such loving devotion'.

This perennial sense of continuity at St Helen's was strengthened by the appointment of Professor Jukes to the Council of Governors. Professor Jukes's grandmother had been Miss Hilda Rowland Brown, the middle sister of the founding five. In November 1983, yet another foundation stone was laid. This time, Mr Lund, Chairman of the Finance Committee, laid the stone for a new Junior School building. In the following year, the Lund Building was opened. Its new library, planned by Miss Leader, was named after the retiring Chairman of the Council of Governors, Lady Habakkuk, who was described by Miss Leader as 'sympathetic, concerned and knowledgeable'. She was succeeded by Miss Ann Kennedy, a long-time friend to the school and to its head. Also retiring in 1984 were Miss Taylor, art teacher for 30 years and Miss Sandbach, music teacher for an unrivalled 42 years. After 15 years as head of LSH Mrs Babbedge left, to be succeeded by Mrs Gosling.

On 10th May 1985, 'Bricks Leader', who had survived an entire two years without supervising the laying of a single foundation stone, welcomed Miss Mackenzie to the school and oversaw her laying a stone for the next new building. This was to become The Kennedy Building – opened the following February and providing much-needed classrooms and an entire floor for the computer studies department. St Helen's was ahead of its time in recognising the need for this facility.

Little St Helen's staff: (L-R) Mrs Babbedge, Mrs Warrick, Miss Woolf, Mrs McCallin, Miss Grainge, Mrs Morrill, 1980.

Laying of the Kennedy Building foundation stone, May 1985.

concerns. She remembered when someone's child had been ill, was concerned when a house move was proving difficult and she thanked people. It was natural, therefore, under such leadership, for all to want to do their best for the pupils. Miss Leader's many friends, former members of staff, and former pupils, value her for her clear-sightedness, her sense of irony and the absurd, her warmth and unfailing enthusiasm for all that is good, true and beautiful, especially the English language, and the fineness of her spirit. Living less than a mile from the school, she remains as interested in St Helen's and its girls, past and present, as ever. Her place in its roll of honour is assured and is indelible in its affections.

'We made many close friendships and confided a lot in each other. Some of my fondest memories are of the imaginative parties we had. We loved dancing either like Madonna or Michael Jackson … Our overseas school trips were also unforgettable.'

NATASHA RODIKIS PRESVYTIS (1986)

The Kennedy Building was the last of Miss Leader's construction projects. She retired in the summer of 1986 after 32 years. Dr Baker also retired from the school at this time but, tragically, he was to have only a few months to enjoy his new freedom with his wife before a sudden decline into illness and an early death. In addition, Frau Gunhild von Berlepsch, for 30 years an extraordinary teacher of German, and June Leader's close friend who retired simultaneously, also fell ill and died within months. She was an unforgettable character, full of warmth, wisdom and dry humour and was mourned and sorely missed. Miss Leader bore the double blow of losing two people so dear to her with characteristic stoicism and wisdom, expressed with honesty and candour. The support of the St Helen's community to which she had given so much for so long was loyal and warmly reciprocated. June the Builder became June the Gardener, June the Mentor, Counsellor and Friend.

As a headmistress she was remarkable in all kinds of ways but, perhaps, most notably for her relationships with those who served under her. It is probably true to say that every member of staff – cooks, groundsmen, house staff, teachers, administrative staff – all felt they had an individual relationship with her. She was genuinely interested in everyone and in their personal

The Kennedy Building, c.1986.

Memories of Junior School – *Anne Wyman (Junior School teacher, 1967–1991)*

Miss Leader's time as Headmistress was an interesting period for Junior School. Both Miss Leader and Miss Paul, the recently appointed Head of Junior School, recognised the need to adapt teaching and administrative methods to suit changes in thinking and lifestyles, while retaining the core values that made St Helen's such a special place.

We tried to make learning interesting and enjoyable and many will remember the wide range of outings and activities this involved. Throughout the year there were visits to most of the major museums. Popular items were standing on the 'earthquake floor' in the Geological Museum, the summer boat trip to Greenwich and the guided tours of Kew Gardens. Miss Paul also began the annual field trips to St Briavels – a highlight of the 2A year.

Sarah Kirchheimer (1997) remembers, 'For 2A, spring term was devoted to the St Briavels trip. I remember the trip as a great adventure; for most of us it was the longest we had ever been away from home on our own …

I have found my St Briavels diary, a work of art which took all term to create … The days followed a fairly regimented format: each morning we would leave our rooms and assemble downstairs. We would have prayers, led by Miss Paul, then move to the dining room for breakfast. Each day consisted of a morning and afternoon activity. We walked along the River Wye to the pottery at Brockweir, visited Tintern Abbey, a dairy farm, the Forest of Dean, a saw-mill, Chepstow Castle, and a sheep farm.

In the evenings we had a talk about the Forest of Dean (with slides!), one about Love Spoons (with spoons!), and on our last

Girls playing outside Claremont.

night a trip to see the Severn Bore. After supper we all sat in the common room to write up our diaries, then were read a story before being sent up to bed. Sadly the trips ceased soon after our visit [in 1989]. I remember the trip with great fondness; even though my diary seems to be littered with "everybody got very wet" and "it was very cold", my overriding memory is of an adventure which I greatly enjoyed.'

As the school grew, it needed more accommodation, so first the old Junior Hall was demolished and the new Lund Building opened in 1984, followed later by the Mackenzie Building, opened in 1990. This was built on what had been a tree-fringed playing area, much loved by the younger ones who liked to build their grass camps there, as Bhavika Nesbitt (Patel, 1997) recalls: 'Before

Junior School girls at work in the 1950s (top) and the 1990s (bottom).

St Briavels trip, 1990s.

rehearsals, the excitement of seeing everyone finally costumed, the occasional worry as to whether the rain would hold off. One year there had to be a dash through relentless rain to the RBH, fervently hoping no one's costume would get too wet.

At the end of the Christmas term would come the Carol Concert. Other ends of term were marked by House netball, rounders and swimming. Towards the end of June, one day would be given over to the House Art Competition. Every entry received a careful review from the judge. There was always an impressive display of widely varying talents. Inevitably, not everyone agreed with the judge's final decisions, but the aim was to emphasise how much everyone's contribution was valued.

Junior School's main charity efforts were focused on Calendar Sale and the fun day at the end of the summer when each House organised various fund-raising activities for UNICEF.

the Mackenzie Building was built, we used to play "camps" – our first dip into the world of commerce. The currency was handfuls and skirtfuls of grass – you could buy anything ... Every Spring Term, we would race out at first break to get a tree which would be yours until the end of term ... We would follow the gardeners around and ask them when the grass was going to be cut, so you could gauge when the next "currency" would be available.' The new building also meant the demolition of the Cottage, used to house a classroom and the old library.

Miss Paul initiated the change from formal Speech Day to the summer pageant, built around a different theme each year, with each form making its own contribution to the performance, and everything linked by songs and dances. One remembers the outdoor

Inevitably, as we approached the 1990s, the educational scene was undergoing more changes. Computer lessons appeared on the timetable and the introduction of SATs affected the planning of the curriculum. Several of us who had taught together for many years reached retirement age and a new era began under new leadership. It says a lot for the St Helen's ethos that we look back on our time there with pleasure, and the friendships forged are still a firm link between us.

Memories of Boarding

Boarders have been part of St Helen's life since its first term when a little girl was accepted as a boarder. Until around 1918, there were a number of 'home boarders' whose parents lived overseas and who remained at the school during holidays, some not seeing their parents for seven years. This created a homely, family feeling amongst the boarders as Teddy Fouraces, a St Helen's boy from 1903 to 1907, wrote: 'we felt Miss Rowland Brown was our foster mother and we were all devoted to her'.

Boarding before World War Two is described in 'The First Eighty Years' as being 'monastic'; girls were not allowed outside the school grounds unescorted until they were seniors, although there were plenty of after school and weekend activities to keep the boarders entertained. Life for the boarders was not as comfortable as it is today, as Pearl Stewart-Black (1928) described: 'Our washing arrangements were spartan to a degree – cold water in our china jugs, often frozen in winter (I don't remember cans of hot water until School House), and the rules were that we must strip to the waist to wash.'

By the 1950s, there was a large boarding community, housed in Gables for the Junior boarders, Middle House for the Fourth Forms, Longworthe for the Lower Fifth and School House for the Upper Fifth and Sixth Forms.

Gables' housemistress was Miss 'Hoppy' Haines, whom Rosalind Carreck (1964) remembers as 'kind-hearted, but she did get flustered and occasionally lose her temper'.

'When I was boarding in Gables and in one of the dorms on either side of "Hoppy's" room, we had to get out of bed at 6.00 am and stand up while Radio 4 played the National Anthem on royal birthdays, before being allowed to get back into bed until the bell went. I still stand up whenever I hear the National Anthem, to this day.'

SALLY FLEMING (POLLOTT, 1973)

In my first term as a boarder in the Gables, I shared Room 4 ... On the last night of the summer term in 1954 some girls had already gone home but a few of us remained and after "Hoppy" Haines had done her rounds, we hit on the idea of doing "flying leaps" off the mantelpiece onto my bed. All went well until we realised that the mantelpiece was coming away from the wall! We hastily pushed it back and decided it was time to settle down. I've often wondered whether it still remains in an upright position!'

LIS RUSHTON (BRANDON, 1959)

Middle House was also the home of the San, in the charge of Sister Cook, 'a battle-axe with a formidable reputation ... Her bark was worse than her bite and her eyes could gleam with laughter, though you could be forgiven for forgetting this when you lined up for her vile cold and cough syrup,' writes Rosalind Carreck, who describes life in Middle House as 'not unlike an Army Boot Camp. We even went on parade before we left for school each morning ... Discipline was strict but I

The Longworthe common room, 1966.

Opposite: Little St Helen's girls going to bed at Ardenlea.

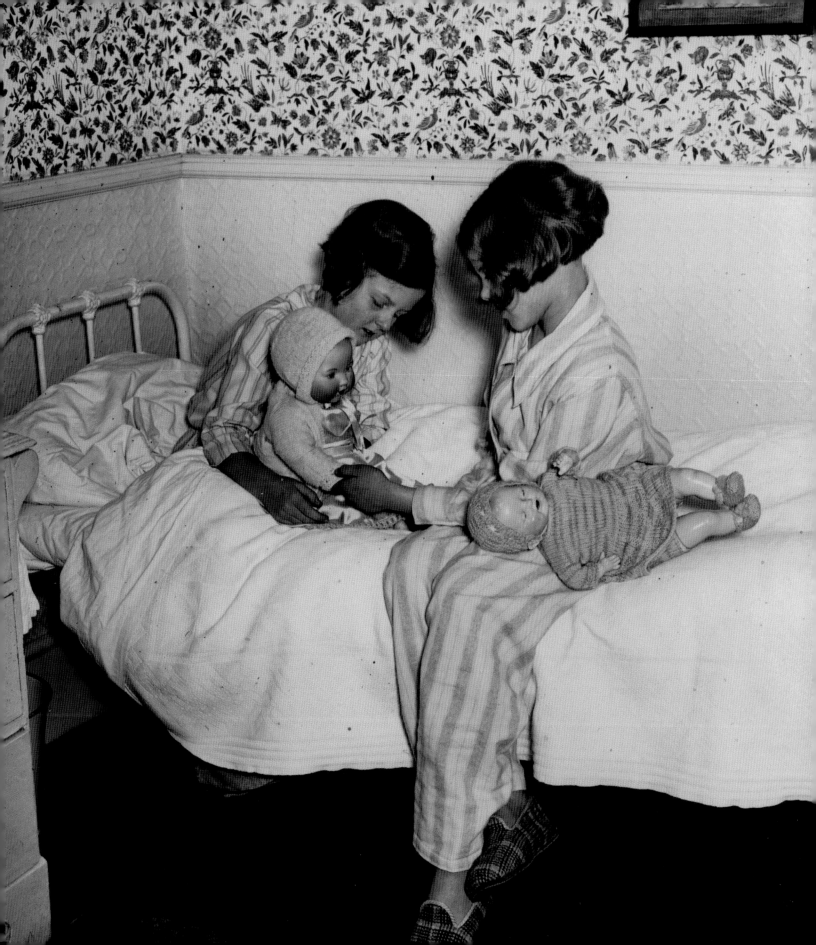

Memories of Boarding

don't remember being unhappy ... Each girl started the term with a maximum number of points which were deducted for ill-made beds, untidy drawers or single hairs left in our brushes...

In the autumn and spring terms, we boarders were part of the great unwashed as we had just two official baths a week – there were no showers ... As for washing our hair, that took place once a fortnight unless we had special dispensation.'

Life for boarders outside the school day was always busy, as Rosalind describes: 'Tennis and extra swimming in the summer, gym club in the winter, music and drama rehearsals; everything had to be fitted in around prep. But best of all were Saturday evenings.

Saturday evenings meant dancing to a record player in the gym ... Occasionally we had a cultural evening – a violin recital for example.' Ingrid Roscoe (Hargreaves-Allen,

Gwyer House Party, 1980s.

1962) remembers, 'Weekends were times to be savoured. On Saturday evenings we donned our best clothes, backcombed our hair and applied judicious mascara before joining all the other boarders in the Gym, where we danced with one another ... We savoured Sunday evenings, when a teacher generously gave her time and read to us in Middle House.' Mary Corrall (1955) recalls, 'Sunday afternoon walks, stopping off at a day girl's house for tea, and ballroom dancing in the old hall on a Saturday evening – I learnt the tango there!'

Boarding numbers have seen a decline in recent decades. Louise Molyneux (Bater, 1993) writes, 'I think my time as a boarder really spanned a transition ... By the time I reached the Sixth Form in 1990 boarding had changed a lot. There were far fewer of us for starters. Mackenzie [a Sixth Form boarding house since the late 1960s] had been demolished,

A boarders' group photo, 1949.

School House had been converted into classrooms, Gwyer [previously Middle House, renamed in 1971 after the Chairman of the first Board of Governors] had been refurbished so that everyone had either a single or a double room. With changing boarding staff the whole atmosphere had relaxed – some of us "old timers" reckoned the younger girls didn't realise they had it so good!' When she joined Gables in 1984, Louise remembers: 'The housemistress ran a tight ship: only five items on top of your chest of drawers; beds made with hospital corners; rotas that decreed I could have a bath on a Monday, Wednesday and Friday ... We had assembly on a Saturday morning, followed by shoe cleaning and then the highlight of the week: a shopping trip to Northwood dressed in a skirt and school blazer accompanied by a teacher to buy sweets in "Top Tuck". We went to chapel in the RBH on a Sunday morning and had compulsory letter writing sessions in the afternoon ... When I look back now it seems archaic but it is the way things were (and I think that is the way they had been for some time). And we did have fun.'

In 1995, as boarding numbers continued to fall, Gables was closed as a boarding house, followed by Longworthe in 2001, when the now much smaller boarding community became one, housed in Gwyer. Eight years later, the last boarders would leave, ending a unique aspect of the school that has enriched the community and given us so many traditions from Strawberry Tea to Spot Supper.

A midnight feast – *Johanna McEvedy (Forsyth, 1978)*

It was the summer of '76 and we were in VA and boarded in School House. Five of us shared a dormitory, the nearest one to the door of the Sixth Form Common Room and the housemistress' sitting room.

It was about 9 o'clock in the evening – we had 'lights out' then, believe it or not. We felt hungry and wide awake, and someone suggested, half-jokingly, how nice a Chinese would be! This rapidly took on possibilities: there was a small takeaway on the corner of Green Lane. Two of us volunteered for the mission; money was collected; we put on jeans and tee-shirts, with dressing gowns on top and set off.

We crept past the housemistress' door into the darkened Common Room, where we left our dressing gowns, down the stairs and out of the front door. A few minutes later we were sauntering casually down the road.

Twenty minutes later we were back, two bulging, steaming and rather pungent carrier bags between us. In through the front door, up the stairs, into the Common Room, dressing gowns on, three steps forward ... disaster struck! The door into the landing opened and light streamed in, outlining the housemistress' figure ... 'What do you think you are doing?'

She didn't see the bags; grateful for my dressing gown, I stood with them hidden behind its skirt. 'We ... er ... were revising. In the far common room.' This worked! There had recently been cases of illicit revision. Perhaps my 'goody-goody' image made this credible.

She unbent slightly. 'Off to bed with you. At once.'

She hadn't switched on the Common Room light so we were able to shuffle our bags down behind one of the chairs. She stood aside as we scurried past. Giggling almost hysterically, we fell back into the dorm. The others were amused but concerned: what about the food?

We gave it ten minutes or so, dashed back into the Common Room and hurtled back with the still-steaming bags. Triumph! We fell on the contents; only then did we realise we didn't actually have anything to eat the delicious cargo with. Tissues and flannels as plates, fingers and even the odd toothbrush as cutlery, it all tasted delicious.

Of course, we didn't dare switch on a light, so clearing up afterwards was necessarily perfunctory and the morning revealed the floor covered in bits of rice. I can't remember now how we disposed of the wrappers, and can only say that we did completely get away with it!

Memories of Boarding

Spot Supper – *Rosalind Carreck (1964)*

Spot Supper was the boarders' end of term feast, so eat your hearts out Hogwarts, hang onto your hats St Trinians, for here's a real taste of boarding at St Helen's.

In the dim and distant past, cloths were used on the dining tables of St Helen's. If you stained the cloth, you paid a fine and these monies funded Spot Supper. By the time I arrived, formica had taken over, but the tradition lived on and was remembered in the song we sang as we filed into the School House dining-room:

Spot Supper, July 1973.

A spot on the table-cloth!
The cloth that was fair to see,
And you have to pay a fine
That the merrier we may be.

There was a tremendous buzz of expectation. Miss Mackenzie and members of staff sat at the top table. Dr Baker was seated on Miss Mackenzie's right, the only man attending the proceedings.

The school cooks did us proud, but as the plates were cleared away, we began to rhythmically pound the tables. It was time for the speeches, led by Dr Baker. He was always amusing, and we banged the tables in appreciation because we were so fond of him.

Now it was the new girls' turn. They were terrified because they'd been told they had to eat a bar of soap as an initiation ritual. It didn't happen, of course, but everyone practised, me included! Then it was the school-leavers' turn. The banging on the tables shook the room as the sixth-formers' jokes grew thick and fast until, at last, Miss Mackenzie was forced to calm the proceedings before the piano struck up and the School Songs began.

And what songs they were, most of them adapted from the Harrow School Song Book. The words might seem banal, but we roared out our parts, and all of us remember those rousing tunes:

St Helen! St Helen!
Empress and Saint, Oh Helen!
To all in need
A friend indeed,
Thy praise still is ringing — St Helen! St Helen!
(St Helen, the School Song)

At last the great feast ended. Miss Mackenzie said grace and we stood to sing 'Good night Ladies', our hearts full of warmth for the school and happy expectation of the holidays to come.

The school's last boarders will undoubtedly remember their time in Gwyer fondly. The atmosphere is very much that of a large family, where lifelong friendships have been formed, as boarders from 2009 testify:

'Gwyer has embraced me like no other place and my friends and the staff here have made everything easier.'

JESSICA CHENG

'I will never forget Gwyer, my first home in the UK, and all the amazing boarders I have lived with.'

GABY CHAN

'When I first arrived, my body shook with nervousness as I was welcomed at the door by Mrs Wooldridge. She gave me a wide grin and said, "Welcome to your new home." At that point I felt like running out the door. Today, I believe that the best decision I ever made was not to.'

ANOUSKA CHELLIAH

'Here, I have understood the meaning of home. A home should be made of the people who you trust and love. All the marvellous girls here have made the boarding house a home for me.'

SHARON SIN

'I know that I will always remember boarding in Gwyer and treasure the many special friendships made with people I have met here. I'll always be grateful to the girls who, albeit equally as homesick as me, were ever-ready to lend a listening ear or a shoulder to cry on.'

ADELINE LOH

This family atmosphere has been a defining part of the boarding, and indeed St Helen's, experience throughout the years, as Pam Witterick's, the current Registrar and an integral part of school life for many years, recollections reflect: 'My association with St Helen's started more than 25 years ago when I was asked by a friend, Mrs Gloria Clifford, who couriered boarders to and from airports, stations and on medical visits, if I could help. At that time there were over 200 boarders ... some of whom lived as far afield as New Zealand, Australia, Brazil, Hong Kong, America or Europe ... Never did I think that this invitation would lead to such an interesting chapter of my life.

To share the girls' excitement at going home at the end of term ... was very special. I got to know many boarders through these trips as well as taking them to their guardians for V-Sats, or London and elsewhere on medical visits.

Over the years I have seen the school grow from strength to strength and am now welcoming daughters of boarders and other Old Girls into the school.

I feel privileged to have had the opportunity to live "the St Helen's experience".'

The school's last boarders, 2009.

Broader Horizons

Kate Ogden

The last decades of the 20th century saw significant changes in the world of education, with GCSEs replacing O Levels in 1986, the introduction of the National Curriculum two years later and the arrival of national league tables in 1992, creating a greater transparency and focus on performance and examination achievement. Opportunities for women continued to open up with more going to university and pursuing a wide range of careers.

Dr Yvonne Burne and Miss Mackenzie.

This was also a time of great change for St Helen's. On Miss Leader's retirement, the Deputy Head, Mrs Sheila Nash, acted as interim Head for a year prior to the arrival of Dr Yvonne Burne. In her 1987 Speech Day report, Mrs Nash referred to some of the challenges in her year of office: 'The theme for this year's magazine was New Beginnings, not exactly prophetic but certainly indicative, for last September girls in VB began work on the new examination, the General Certificate of Secondary Education. They will be judged at the end of their two-year course "not only on their performance in written papers, but on the work they do during their course" ... Such a radical change in approach has had its repercussions at all levels in Senior School ... but meanwhile it has set a challenge which is exciting and rewarding ... Next September St Helen's will begin a new era when we welcome Dr Burne as our Headmistress. Once again the pattern of school life will rearrange itself to form a new design.'

There is little doubt that succeeding a Headmistress such as Miss Leader, who had inspired such respect and devotion, would not be an easy task. But Dr Burne joined the school with great ambitions for the future and for the school's place in a rapidly changing world.

Writing about her time as Headmistress in 1995, Dr Burne summed up what her vision had been: 'When I joined St Helen's ... eight years ago I had four key objectives:

PHAB

Rolf Harris visit, PHAB week, 1998.

Girls have been taking part in PHAB (Physically Handicapped Able Bodied) for many years. During the Easter holidays, a group of sixth form girls, along with boys from Merchant Taylors' School look after a group of physically handicapped children at a week-long holiday camp held at Merchant Taylors'.

Preparation for the week's holiday starts months in advance as pupils must raise the funds needed for the week. One particularly memorable fund-raising event is the PHAB Revue. 'I remember being part of a group of girls who performed a dance to Madonna's "Vogue" – we probably looked completely ridiculous but, at the time we didn't seem to mind; it was all part of the spirit of raising enough money for PHAB week, whether or not you were actually helping during the week, whatever it took!' remembers Lauren Osmond (Hill, 1996).

The week is enjoyed immensely by the children and pupil-helpers alike, with a huge variety of trips and activities organised for the campers, which have included days out to London and Chessington World of Adventures, swimming, a disco, and shopping and cinema trips. Whilst it is certainly a tiring week for the helpers and staff involved, it is also a hugely rewarding experience, as one girl described in the 1997 school magazine: 'A week, that felt like a life time and yet went so quickly was suddenly over and we all realised how much we'd learnt about ourselves, each other and life, because school and almost anything else is not comparable to the experiences that you have on PHAB. I feel so privileged to have taken part in a week such as this.'

PHAB week, 1995.

A PHAB outing to the London Eye, 2008.

- The first was to modernise the school;
- The second was to help the pupils to look beyond the confines of school and the local community to Europe and the world beyond;
- Thirdly, I wanted to build on the existing academic traditions to make the quality of teaching and learning as high as possible, and to enable the school to take its place amongst the leading independent schools in the country. The pupils would, I hoped, become ... pleasantly assertive and independently minded young women from a variety of social backgrounds and cultures ... capable of transforming the glass ceiling into a glass floor;
- Lastly, I wanted to preserve the happy and caring quality of the school, and to ensure that the girls retained a sense of service to others; a sense of their duties, as well as of their rights; of self-confidence without self-absorption.'

Challenge of Management, 1993.

Reflecting on her vision, Dr Burne now recalls, 'I had always been driven by trying to give girls every opportunity and ... I really wanted to see education as a whole ... What I wanted to do was to give the girls plenty of opportunities such as exchanges, work experience; I just wanted them to be out and about and having every opportunity they could ... The ethos was lovely and it's still there. It's such a caring, friendly school and I think that's all down to June Leader and to Miss Mackenzie before her, and you would never want to change that.'

As well as pursuing academic excellence, the extra-curricular programme continued to be an integral part of school life and school magazines are full of reports of exciting trips at home and abroad, expeditions, clubs, societies, fund-raising activities, sporting successes, drama and musical performances. The girls of St Helen's were clearly eager to accept new challenges and to take advantage of the wide variety of activities available to them. In a period of technological development and globalisation, Dr Burne was keen that the girls looked to the world beyond, so that they embraced all the opportunities that were opening up whilst at the same time being prepared for the challenges they might meet along the way.

Much energy was put into developing the school's external links both at home and abroad. Closer ties with Merchant Taylors' School were forged, even including the consideration of a physical move to new purpose-built facilities on the Merchant

Taylors' site which did not materialise. Other links (both new and existing) flourished, including joint drama and music productions, the Sixth Form Society, the French Circle, joint careers activities, PHAB and, in September 1991, the inclusion of St Helen's girls in the Combined Cadet Force, with 23 5B girls donning their Army, Navy and RAF uniforms and making the weekly Friday afternoon trip to Merchant Taylors', with ever-increasing numbers joining them in the following years. On St Barnabas' Day 1990, the Head Girl was admitted, together with the Head Boy of Merchant Taylors', as apprentice of the Merchant Taylors' Company, a tradition which continued for several years and which was symbolic of the close links between the two schools.

Links with business and industry were also fostered to enhance teaching strategies and prepare the girls for the world beyond school. Staff were encouraged to take up work placements to gain first-hand experience of industry. The careers department expanded, with all girls benefitting from work experience after their GCSEs and involvement with the 'Take Your Daughters to Work' scheme lower down the school.

Dr Burne was acutely aware of change on the European political and economic landscape and several initiatives were introduced to ensure that the girls would be prepared for the

(continued on p. 97)

Drama – *Danni Sinclair (Drama teacher and Head of Upper School)*

'Masque of Empire', 1911.

The Rowland Brown sisters could not have imagined how drama would develop from the school play and occasional performance in the classroom into an examined subject in its own right. The uptake at GCSE and in the sixth form continues to grow. In recent years more girls have opted to read Drama at university or to enrol in one of London's drama schools, in the hope of following in the steps of Old Girl Patricia Hodge.

Miss Hodge progressed from starring in school productions, such as 'The Beggar's Opera' and 'As You Like It', to the West End stage, television and cinema. In 2001 she returned to the Rowland Brown stage to perform in 'Reflection of St Helen's' which was a huge success, although she apparently commented it was more daunting than performing at the National!

The vast array of plays produced at St Helen's over the years illustrates not only the versatility and subject knowledge of the teaching staff but also represents changes in society and education. Shakespeare has been popular when it comes to productions. St Helen's has produced 'The Merchant of Venice', 'Twelfth Night', 'As You Like It' and 'A Midsummer Night's Dream' (twice) and 'The Tempest' featured three times in the last century. St Helen's has, in recent years, entered the School Shakespeare Festival and performed 'The Taming of the Shrew' at the Ryan Theatre.

Currently, the examination boards encourage the promotion of modern playwrights, often dealing with sensitive issues. In 1998, Alan Allkins produced 'Two Weeks with the Queen' by Mary Morris (not our current Head). The play portrays a family's coming to terms with their child's leukaemia, whilst 'Haroun and the Sea of Stories', written by Salman Rushdie, was an innovative piece of drama, exploring the importance of the age-old art of storytelling.

In the 1960s and 1970s, Gilbert and Sullivan light operas, such as 'The Pirates of Penzance', 'HMS Pinafore' and 'The Yeoman of the Guard' were very well received. The declamatory style is less appealing to a modern audience and musicals such as

*I always threw myself into whatever drama productions were on. I had the pleasure of being in such shows as "The Rebels of Gas Street", "Anne of Green Gables", "Grease" and "Salad Days". I was desperate to also be in "Guys and Dolls", but that was in my 6A year and my mother reminded me I was actually at school to pass exams, not to be on stage. I will always be grateful for the experiences I got from being in these shows.'

JOANNA LAWLOR (TWINING, 1994)

'Les Misérables', 'Return to the Forbidden Planet' and 'Guys and Dolls' have taken over the musical slot.

St Helen's enjoys a special bond with Merchant Taylors' School and many a romance has blossomed during rehearsals. Musicals have become a popular annual joint production, with the venue now alternating between the two schools. 'We Will Rock You!' in 2008 was a sell-out and a showcase for the enormous talent of the performers. The spectacular set was designed by Kathryn Archer, ably assisted by Year 9 who enjoyed a design project on costumes for 'the Bohemians'. Historically, all costumes were home-spun. 'I remember spending hours hand-sewing my ruffles and buckles for "Iolanthe". I refused to wear yet another curtain!' remembers Rebecca Hershman (Baxter, 1964). Mrs Valery Cowley (English, 1969–1989) recalls the skills of one memorable wardrobe mistress in the 1960s who was also an excellent Geography teacher: 'Marjorie Dover made costumes out of blackout curtains for "The Insect Play" but was alarmed to discover that the fragile material had to stand up to active drill by the insects.' Margaret MacIntosh's ability to create costumes out of nothing was illustrated by the wardrobe she fashioned for Toad in 'The Wind in the Willows'.

'We Will Rock You!', 2008.

Costume-making and set construction have always relied heavily on the goodwill and hidden talents of staff and girls. Miss Taylor, Head of Art from 1954 to1984, recalls, 'The Drama produced by June Leader, and various other members of staff, gave us hard work and a good deal of enjoyment. We were responsible for scenery and make-up; there were lively opportunities for imaginations and skills.' Whether it is the box set for 'The Boyfriend', masks for 'Animal Farm' or rushes and plants for 'The Wind in the Willows', girls and staff have enthusiastically given up their time to assist the audience in suspending their disbelief.

The technical aspects allow girls who are not natural performers to enjoy the excitement and thrill of theatre. In 2008, St Helen's employed a theatre technician and the Technical Club has encouraged many girls to learn about all backstage elements vital to any successful production.

Speech and Drama continues to be an important part of the extra-curricular programme. Although no longer referred to as diction or elocution, where girls were drilled in 'How Now Brown Cow', the trend is towards vocal clarity. Society celebrates diversity, reflected by the trend towards promoting regional accents. Excellent communication skills have always been a quality of St Helen's pupils and drama will always be an important part of moulding girls into confident, charming and articulate individuals.

'The Tempest', 1966.

> *'I remember the excitement, playing Sandy in "Grease", when ... the Pink Ladies [visited the] costume cupboard. It was a treasure trove! I think I costumed myself for "Calamity Jane", "Fame" and "Phantom of the Opera" before actually finding anything that Sandy might have worn!'*
>
> JESSICA SIMS (PLUMRIDGE, 1996)

Dr Yvonne Burne with HRH Princess Alice at the opening of the Mackenzie Building, 2nd May 1990.

many opportunities it was anticipated would arise from a united Europe. In the summer of 1991, two 6B girls were offered the chance of taking part in the European Work Experience programme, working at Marks & Spencer in Lille. This programme grew to include other companies in France, Germany and Spain in subsequent years.

Other activities that girls were encouraged to participate in included the European Youth Parliament and, from October 1994, the Model United Nations to further their awareness of worldwide issues. 'The purpose of our visits, at home and abroad, is to try to produce confident, well-informed citizens, able to make the most of life in every way and who should be fortified by the tolerance and co-operation imbibed through joint experience

Ernst & Young business game, July 1995.

Opposite: 'Cabaret', 1997.

and community living,' was Dr Burne's message at Speech Day in 1995.

Further afield, Dr Burne visited the Far East in 1994 to build relationships in a part of the world that was emerging as an important player in the global economy, as she reported: '... my whole experience of Hong Kong and Taipei was stimulating and positive beyond belief. I had planned to meet existing parents, the parents of former pupils and old girls. I wanted to spread St Helen's name in the Far East and to attract intelligent and lively girls from the families of expatriates and from China, Hong Kong and Taiwan ... I left convinced that we must teach our own young people more of the language, culture and history of the Far East and that this will be essential if St Helen's girls are to meet the challenges of the 21st century. Our young women are all likely to be living in a European context, but possibly with the Far East increasingly in the driving seat!'

As pupil numbers grew and the curriculum changed, the development of the school's buildings continued. In September 1989, Little St Helen's expanded to include girls rising five, whilst Junior School now included girls from seven rather than eight years old. This meant that more accommodation for Junior School was required, and so began the next stage of building work. The new Mackenzie Building, with its purpose-built teaching rooms for science, technology and music as well as additional classroom space, was opened by HRH Princess Alice, returning to St Helen's after over 30 years, on 2nd May 1990. 'I remember wanting desperately to be chosen to present Princess Alice with flowers and that this privilege went to the only girl in Junior School

(continued on p. 101)

CCF – Tricia Cullen (Flying Officer)

The CCF contingent has gone from strength to strength since girls were first able to join in 1991. There are now as many as 150 girls who put on their uniforms and board the bus for Merchant Taylors' every Friday after school. This shows a great commitment at the end of a busy week and is testament to their dedication and enthusiasm.

The Army section remains the largest but recruitment into the Navy and RAF has grown each year. It has been good to see female cadets in the most senior NCO positions in all three sections.

Field Days have always been a great way to spend a day, covered in mud on an Army Training Ground; bobbing about on the sea at Portsmouth or just cruising through the air in a small Grub training aircraft. Of course, officers take a full part and are expected to do everything cadets do.

One female officer clearly remembers being in a forest in Hampshire where 'Go Ape' was the highlight of the day. Swinging through the trees at 60 feet off the ground, leaping across open spaces into cargo nets suspended in the branches, abseiling to the ground and landing with a resounding bump! She is glad to have done it but not again, please!

Summer camps in July are also adventurous times. The Navy girls experience life on a battleship, RAF girls take a trip in a Chinook helicopter and Army girls wield weapons, sometimes knee deep in mud. The special day of the CCF year is Inspection Day involving a re-formed CCF Band to play along to marching and drill.

'Getting the coach to Merchant Taylors' was a highlight of the week. There was a real buzz when the coach arrived … The assault courses, camouflage paint, etc, soon undid any glamourising we had done! Army camps, shooting, getting shouted at on parade and other activities were certainly all great for character-building!'

AMY CALAM (1998)

'Even though I've had to give up my Friday evenings, being part of the CCF has given me the opportunity to do things that not many people can claim to have done. Whether it was going on the summer camp in the middle of nowhere or shooting blanks, I've been given a vast number of opportunities and had a great time seizing them!'

LAURA WILSON (CURRENT PUPIL)

One of the most memorable events of 2009 was a visit by two Gurkha soldiers, wearing their VCs and accompanied by lawyer Martin Howe. Over 500 girls and staff, including all our cadets, packed the Hall to hear him speak about the Gurkhas' Campaign for Justice. You could have heard a pin drop until the final standing ovation to honour and respect two real heroes.

Another big occasion is the Anzac Parade at the Cenotaph in April. How proud we are to march along with our Australian and New Zealand comrades. The service in Westminster Cathedral brings a memorable day to an end.

There is no better way for young people to learn about themselves. In a society which no longer values the innate skills of young people it is so good to see all that they achieve. Any time I hear adults grumble about 'young people today', I leap in and tell them all about our cadets and the guts and determination they show in the face of danger and challenge. Long live the CCF at St Helen's, a jewel in its crown.

CCF inspection day, 1998.

International Links – *Ed Terris (Head of Modern Languages)*

The Italian Exchange, 2008.

Exchanges between St Helen's girls with students from educational establishments throughout the world have developed over the last 20 years and have been an important addition to the curriculum by raising language and cultural awareness. Many of those taking part in the exchanges go on to study a language at university: 'I remember going to Goslar on an exchange. Although German was a hard language to learn, I enjoyed the challenge of the complicated grammar and went on to study German Language and Literature at Leeds University ... and have been lucky enough to use German in my work since,' writes Angela Lawrence (1991).

Successful exchanges have taken place to schools in Toulouse, Madrid, Goslar, Heidelberg, Vicenza, Hatsushiba and Tokyo. Many girls keep in contact with their exchange partner. These links have come about through various means: Mme Cone set up the exchange to L'Annonciation, in Toulouse in 1990 and this has continued almost every year since. Girls have been entertained lavishly with *foie gras* and champagne. The exchange to St Raphael Gymnasium in Heidelberg, which was preceded for several years by the exchange to Goslar, began in October 1995 when a group of 15 pupils from St Helen's and Merchant Taylors' travelled to Germany for a week, accompanied by then Head of German, Mr Ulrich Schreiber. The second exchange took place in 1998 and involved 17 girls from St Helen's. Spanish groups, primarily from Year 10, have been going successfully to the Colegio Altair in Madrid every year since 1998.

The recent exchanges to Japan evolved from an impromptu visit to St Helen's by the headmaster of the Hatsushiba High School in 2001. From a small beginning, we have sent girls every year to Japan. Another link started from a contact made with a high school in Tokyo. Mrs Ishikawa accompanies the group and the girls enjoy a variety of activities from travelling on the bullet train to martial arts and visits to palaces, gardens and temples. In 2007, Mrs O'Hagan set up a link with the Liceo Classico Pigafetta in Vicenza.

Sixth form students are encouraged to do work experience abroad. In 1991 Mrs Gerry set up a work experience programme in Lille. Over the years about 50 girls took part in the programme working in a variety of capacities in offices and shops. Many will affectionately remember their 'stage' in bakeries and the Match supermarket. Since 2006 we have used an accompanied work experience programme. Work has been varied from working in department stores, chemists, sports centres, fashion outlets and even dog grooming. Lizzie Tym learned a whole new French vocabulary when she worked in the grooming parlour. Sixth form German students have been going to the department store, Kaufhof, in Heidelberg for many years whilst Spanish students have been involved in work experience in Seville. In Japan, students have worked for schools' English departments as teaching assistants.

The Japanese Exchange, 2008.

Patricia Hodge opening Gwyer House, 11th October 1991.

called Alice. Many days were spent by the rest of us whining to our parents that they had not had the foresight to call us Alice. We placed some objects in a time capsule behind the plaque on the ground floor of the building so that if the building was ever demolished people in the future would have an idea of what life had been like ... On the day of the opening we had to stand outside, lining the pathway, being as quiet as mice ... Later, when Princess Alice walked round, she actually stopped and talked to me. It was the highlight of my entire day!' recalled one sixth form student in 1999.

The new Junior School building was opened just as Miss Paul, a much-loved teacher who had been at St Helen's for 24 years, retired as Head of Junior School. Upon her retirement in July 1990, Miss Leader wrote, 'Like many quiet, apparently unassertive, people Miss Paul has much determination which has always been directed towards seeing that those for whom she was responsible were given the very best that education could offer, not simply in the classroom but in the care with which children at school need to be surrounded ... Nobody can sum up or assess the contribution of one person to the welfare of a school. We can, however, recognise selflessness, generosity, kindness in a world ... which puts its present emphasis on "getting ahead in life".'

Changes also took place in Senior School with classrooms in the main school building converted back into a hall, now known as Old Hall, during the summer of 1990. The following summer, a new sixth form area was created in School House, complete with teaching rooms, a common room and a study area to accommodate the growing sixth form. Gwyer was also refurbished that year as sixth form boarding facilities and was opened on 11th October 1991 by Old Girl Patricia Hodge.

Mrs Marilyn Gerry in the language laboratory, c.1994.

Changes to the curriculum meant that all girls studied three sciences up to GCSE, creating a demand for more laboratories and, on 12th May 1995, the new science wing was opened by Professor Heinz Wolff, Founder of the Brunel Institute for Engineering. The new wing was named after Mrs Valerie Howarth who had retired as Head of Science in July 1992 after 19 years at St Helen's and who had sadly passed away a year after her retirement. She had greatly expanded the teaching of science since her arrival in 1973 and had to a great extent influenced the school's 'science for all' policy and the decision to create more laboratory space. That same year, the school was greatly saddened by the sudden death of school porter extraordinaire, John Swan, who had been at St. Helen's since 1961.'

Design & Technology had also been introduced to the curriculum, starting in a portacabin next to the science building

'Never have I been anywhere with as many acronyms as at St Helen's. One hoped you weren't passing the RBH (Rowland Brown Hall), wearing your GKs (Green Knickers), whilst eating TK (Tomato Ketchup), heading to the K Building (Kennedy), or going to J School (Junior).'

JOANNA LAWLOR (TWINING, 1994)

'When they say that school days are the happiest of your life, I always thought it was a cliché ... and then I spent 11 year at St Helen's. Looking back, there was so much laughter and happy times that I struggle to have a bad memory ... I loved every year I spent at St Helen's and used to enjoy Open Days when I was filled with great pride at showing prospective pupils around my lovely school.'

KIM FISHMAN (2000)

Chair of Governors, Miss Jennifer Priestley, and Mrs Diana Jefkins planting the Centenary Rose bush, 1999.

in September 1989 – 'Our portacabin was so *avant-garde* that people came to visit it!' recalls Dr Burne – and developing as a subject in subsequent years. During the summer of 1994, the Design & Technology laboratories moved to more permanent premises on the ground floor of the June Leader building, whilst the Art studios moved upstairs. That same summer, a Modern Languages corridor was created in the main school building, incorporating a new language laboratory, funded by the PTA.

Development of the site continued under Mrs Diana Jefkins, who was appointed as the School's Headmistress in 1995, following Dr Burne's move to become Headmistress of the City of London School for Girls. During the summer of 1997, work began on refurbishing Gables, which had been closed as a boarding house two years earlier, to provide new accommodation for Little

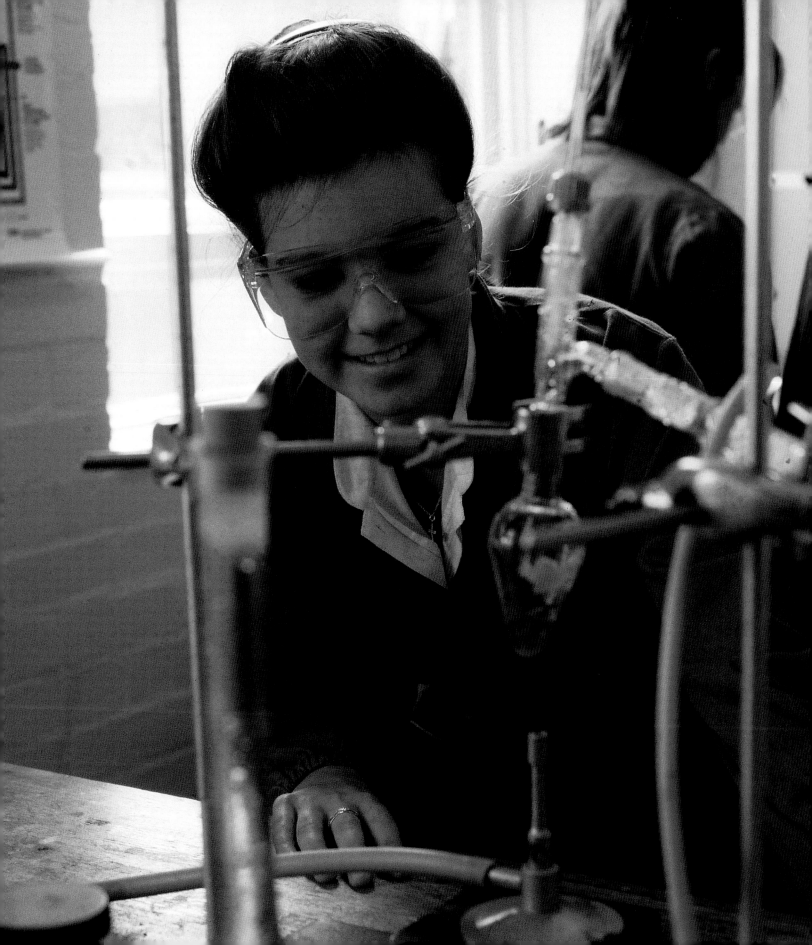

'St Helen's played a major part in not only my life, but my family's life. I was there from 1984 until 1994. Ten extremely happy years. However, the last four years of my time there were fairly unique as I shared them with my mother who was a French teacher. I remember when she came to tell me she had the job. It was the spring of 1990 – that in-between stage of growing out of Middle School but coming into being the youngest in what was Senior School "proper" (Lower Fifth!). She was so happy and I was happy too. But inevitably, as the summer holidays came to a close, and the new term loomed, I began to wonder whether this was such a good thing! School was the one place I could go to every day and not have my parents know my every move … She would see me around the corridors, she would hear things about me from other teachers. She would know if I was in trouble, if I had not handed in my prep … This was very bad news. Very bad news indeed. As it happens, I worried unnecessarily. If I was happy at St Helen's before she joined, I was even happier when we were there together.

When you've been somewhere 10 years, from the ages of 8 to 18, you've done a lot of living within those walls, and a lot of growing up. You watch the years above you leave every year, see them crying in the balcony to "Jerusalem", yet when the day dawns that it's your turn, you can't quite believe the years have gone by. It's your time to shed a tear now. Tears were shed, but we had a bit of celebrating to do too first … We managed to cover most of the teachers' cars in toilet paper, like they were all presents waiting to be unwrapped! We did the tango through the staffroom, en masse. We drove our cars through the grounds, past the RBH, round the K building, and up the path past the gym before we got stopped. We set all the chairs out for assembly, including the Head's table, chairs and lectern, out on the lower lax pitch next to the RBH. And, my personal favourite, we covered up all the portraits of the past Heads with individual photos of members of "Take That". It was harmless fun, but I still remember it … Doesn't quite beat the gorilla-gram that sat on Dr Byrne's knee the year before, but it wasn't far behind.'

JOANNA LAWLOR (TWINING, 1994)

Dear Finder,

MY NAME IS: Kate Cooney

FORM: 7 Shackleton

I have entered this balloon race for charity to celebrate 100 years of the founding of St. Helen's School. I would be very grateful if you would fill in the space below and post this card back to my school, I might win a prize.

Thank you very much.

This balloon was found in:

Area: U.S.A.   Town/Village: OAKTON VIRGINIA U.S.A.

Date: 14 JULY 1999

Centenary birthday party, July 1999.

St Helen's. The girls and staff moved in a year later. The sixth form area was extended to incorporate a new, larger common room and an expanded study area.

The century ended with the school celebrating its centenary with a variety of activities planned for all members of the school community, including pupils, parents, staff and Old Girls. The celebrations were launched in October 1998 with the planting of a commemorative rose and each girl receiving a commemorative mug. Gables was officially opened in the same month by the Chairman of Governors and Old Girl, Miss Jennifer Priestley. Celebrations continued throughout the year, concluding with the Centenary Birthday Party on 11th July 1999.

Looking back at the last year of the century at Speech Day, Mrs Jefkins reflected that, 'The future is full of challenge, but it is also full of opportunity. In our Centenary Year, we have been encouraged both to look back with gratitude and to look forward with enthusiasm ... The School is vibrant and full of life. It retains that strong sense of community which was embodied in the early life of the School. It remains, for all its size and complexity, a family of people, drawn together by common goals.' It was certainly a community ready to take on the challenges and opportunities of the 21st century.

House Arts

Competition between the Senior Houses in drama, music and art has been a long-standing tradition at St Helen's, and the annual House Arts Competition, which replaced the House Drama and Music Competitions that took place on alternate years began in the early 1990s. The competition requires each House to put on an original performance which includes art (in the form of spectacular programmes), dance, drama and music.

The excitement around Senior School is palpable in the last few weeks of the Summer Term. Groups of girls can be seen in every spare corner of the school in break times, lunch times and after school preparing for what many might regard as the highlight of the school year. When the day itself arrives, the rest of Senior School falls silent as everyone can be found in the RBH, cheering on their House at an, at times, ear-splitting volume.

Memories of House Arts certainly stay with the participants as Kim Fishman (2000) recalls, 'Directing Bonington's winning House Arts performance in 1999 was pretty special, when all our hard work and team work paid off'. Kate Bonham's (2008) description captures an experience that truly reflects the spirit of St Helen's, 'For me, St Helen's is summed up by House Arts day. Every single girl in one hall cheering, singing, and stamping their feet in unison in anticipation of each House's performance. House Arts brought together girls from all ages and formed strong bonds between year groups, giving role models to look up to when I was younger, and some great friends years younger than me to pass on my wisdom to as a sixth former directing the performances. The atmosphere in the RBH during that day every year is unforgettable, one of great unity and representative of a strong community which you really felt part of.'

House Arts, 1998.

Little St Helen's – *Gina Gosling (Head of Little St Helen's, 1981–2003)*

I really enjoyed meeting Miss Leader at my interview in January 1981 and, as we talked, the more I wanted to work for her. My imagination raced with the possibilities of working in such a lovely environment, and when the offer did come, I had no hesitation in accepting the post of Head of Little St Helen's and First Form teacher from September 1981.

I visited the school a few times over the next six months and attended Founder's Day Assembly, where Miss Mackenzie addressed the school, capturing the attention of even the youngest children. Penny Marshall, the Head Girl, (later a presenter on 'News at Ten') organised the prefects on stage and led the prayers with such maturity and authority that I had thought she was a member of staff.

There were five classes in Little St Helen's, all of mixed ages. I felt that teaching in academic year groups was educationally more appropriate so began restructuring in September 1982. Some initial reorganisation of classes resulted in two 1A classes for seven year olds, from which girls would transfer to Junior School. 1B1 was a mixed class of older fives and the youngest six year olds. The rest of the six year olds went to 1B2.

A gradual process of redecoration began to transform the inside of the building. Tiling the ground floor toilets in a pretty pink made them look less like public lavatories and, after much pleading with the Bursar, we were supplied with rolls of soft toilet tissue instead of Izal! Central heating was installed. Dark walls and ceilings were repainted white and the hall, stairs and landing were carpeted, making the place look inviting.

When I first started, every teacher had a free half day in exchange for undertaking other duties. Half days off were covered by Mrs McCallin who taught Nature Study on those afternoons. At other times, she looked after the library and soothed the children's grazed knees with her wonderful antiseptic lotion, 'Pink Magic'. She retired in the same year as Miss Leader. In September 1989, the 1A classes moved to the new Mackenzie Building. A full Kindergarten intake of four year olds took their place and, from the following year, there was no longer a need for a mixed-age class. We retained the name Kindergarten until 1994, when we adopted the National Curriculum titles of Reception, Year 1 and Year 2.

Little St Helen's class, 1990s.

Michael Gosling

'In Little Saints we had "indoor" and "outdoor" shoes and had been told that whenever we went out to play or came back into the building we had to change our shoes accordingly … Years afterwards my parents told me that the teachers had informed them that one day there was a fire drill and although everyone was lined up in the playground … I could not be found. Eventually I was located and what was I doing? Changing my shoes of course!'

ANGELA LAWRENCE (1991)

The daily walks to Gables for lunch provided an opportunity to observe the changing seasons. Lunchtime was an important aspect of the children's social education. Good table manners were taught and the pupils were shown the correct way to hold cutlery. Food was prepared and cooked on the premises. Meals were served family style, older children taking it in turns to be head of a table where no member of staff was present. Mixing the age groups at the tables ensured that the youngest children had help so they gained confidence and independence.

In my first few years at St Helen's, May Day was a working day. To make the occasion fun, there was a tradition of holding a Theme

May Day 'Away Day', 1981.

years later, when Mrs Willitts told me that friends of her daughter had really believed at the time that they were in a Jumbo Jet.

Another memorable event was the wonderful Pageant devised by Judi Herman to celebrate the school's 90th Anniversary. On the Friday afternoon of Old Girls' weekend in May 1989, and again on the Saturday, Little St Helen's started the proceedings on the lawn behind Gables with a pastiche devised by Mrs Warrick. Each pupil wore a white Victorian smock (made by an army of sewing mothers).

For the Centenary of the school at its current site in 2002, we held a Victorian Day and smocks were worn again. Visiting historians brought in Victorian desks and set up a school in the Hall. For lunch, the girls packed their own knapsacks for a picnic in the orchard beside Gables. Mrs Warrick, who had retired in 1994, returned to the school to organise Victorian singing games. The Orchard became a magical place for young children, who would look for fairy rings and hear about foxes living nearby.

Annual whole-school outings were a great treat. My favourite trip was to Cassiobury Park, where each year group had a ride on a canal barge, a journey on the miniature train, paddled in the pool, and played on the swings and climbing frames. The last whole-school outing was to Windsor Castle in 1992. As always, the well-behaved children in their boaters elicited compliments from other

Day. In May 1981, the theme was an 'Away Day.' I wore a sari and my classroom was decorated with photographs of and artifacts from Sri Lanka.

The children had designed and made their passports the previous week and staff had planned the itinerary. Nevertheless, even I was taken aback when Miss Woolf, dressed as an air hostess, announced, 'The Jumbo has landed'. This was the signal for everyone to assemble in the Hall, where they were seated, aircraft-style, for Assembly. As each group visited a classroom, passports were stamped. At lunchtime, the girls reassembled in the 'Jumbo Jet' where plated chicken salads were distributed by the stewardesses. The reward for organising these kinds of events came

> *'May Day Bank Holiday was a school day, but ... it was always a themed day and we had to come in fancy dress. I vividly recall one year was "Alice in Wonderland" and I came dressed as Alice. We played games and got to go to Senior School to watch the Disney film in our own cinema!'*
> Bhavika Nesbitt (Patel, 1997)

The 90th birthday pageant outside Gables.

Little St Helen's

Little St Helen's PE class, 1990s.

visitors. Thereafter, year group outings relevant to studies took the place of whole-school ventures.

Raising money for charity usually stemmed from the requests of individual children. In 1998, a sponsored Treasure Hunt raised well over £1,000 for the new children's ward at Harefield Hospital. A sponsored Exercisathon raised £900 for Research into Diabetes in 1992 and in 1995, Mrs Willitts organised a Swimathon which raised a substantial amount for the Asthma Association. Also in 1992, Miss Leader asked if we could raise some money for the Royal School for the Deaf in Margate, of which she was a Governor. She was aware that both of my parents, who were born deaf, had been pupils at the school. I liaised with the teacher who led the children's 'signed singing' choir and it was arranged that they would perform two carols at our Christmas Concert. In the meantime, many girls from Little Saints chose to attend my lunchtime practices to learn the signs and sing 'I'd like to teach the world to sing'. At the Concert, the girls performed this song with the deaf children. It was very moving and a collection raised £400.

In due course, boarding numbers declined and Gables was destined to become the new home for Little St Helen's. It was a privilege to be in a position to decide how the rooms could be restructured to best fit the purpose.

By June 1998, the redevelopment of Gables was complete. I remain most grateful to those pupils and staff for ensuring that the ethos and happy atmosphere was carried from the old school to the new. For the first time in all my years at Little St Helen's, Sports Day was cancelled that year due to rain. This would be the case for the two subsequent years, so the first Sports Day held on the lawns at Longworthe was a novel experience for every child, and for several members of staff, who had joined the school since the move.

In the mid-1980s, council grants were available for the development of conservation areas in schools. Mrs Warrick successfully applied for one and, together with Mr Covey, the Head Gardener, established a spring flower meadow and woodland area. Children loved to wander here at playtimes and, at Coffee Mornings, girls would give visitors a guided tour for 10 pence.

In 2001, architects had drawn up plans for the redevelopment of 75 Green Lane. I was asked to plan for a Nursery intake of three year olds and consider the general organisation of the split-site departments to be established in September 2003 prior to my retirement in July 2003. In September 2002, Miss Chaventré took my place in the Reception Class so that my teaching commitments could be reduced, though I still managed to be involved with reading and writing activities. I had known Jo since she was a member of the Lower Sixth. We kept in touch and I was particularly happy when, in January 2005, she was appointed Head of Little St Helen's.

> '*I was in Little Saints when they first set up the "Nature Area" – a corner of the field that was sectioned off with a border of trees – it was to be an area where the gardeners wouldn't mow the lawn, and we would see what grew there, and what insects and birds would come to it – there were lots of ladybirds!*
>
> *In 1A2, we had a hamster, called Honey – at weekends, we took it in turns to take her home. I think our parents dreaded it but we used to get really excited about it.*'
>
> BHAVIKA NESBITT (PATEL, 1997)

Opposite: Mrs Gina Gosling and Little St Helen's girls.

Uniform

'I haven't worn bottle green for about 10 years since leaving school, but am gradually starting to. I will always think of St Helen's when I wear the colour.'

AMY CALAM (1998)

A sentiment that most Old Girls can relate to, and many will be surprised to discover that green has not always featured so prominently in the uniform. Indeed, when St Helen's was first founded, there was no uniform, except for drill and games when, until 1910, blue woollen jerseys and skirts (well below the knee) with scarlet sailor collars and sashes were worn. In 1910, green made its first appearance in the uniform with a green pleated tunic with girdle being introduced for games, becoming uniform throughout the day, worn over a tussore blouse, in 1913. Two years later, brown overalls started to be worn to protect clothing during games.

By the 1930s the uniform had grown to consist of 'black shoes, black woollen stockings, navy blue coats topped with a green serge hat with the school badge ... Gloves must also be worn except in the summer when blazers were worn with Panama hats surrounded by the green and gold striped petersham ribbon' with cotton summer tunics, which developed into a dress with short sleeves. By this time the pleated tunic had been replaced by a green serge tunic without

The prefects in uniform, 1949.

pleats, described in 'The First Eighty Years' as 'a source of great pride, being in our eyes more elegant than the regulation pleated green tunic adopted by so many schools'. The upper sixth were allowed to wear a navy blue skirt with the school blouse and a green and gold striped tie instead of the tunic.

In 1935, green cloaks were introduced, as Dinah West (Conington, 1945) remembers: 'They were made of slightly rough tweed and sage green in colour ... They arrived in large cardboard boxes and given to us in the big hall.' Cloaks continued to be worn by boarders until the 1990s.

Following World War Two, Ann Hinds (Popham, 1955) describes the uniform thus: 'In winter, green tunics, cream blouses, green V-neck pullover with gold stripes round the neck, cloaks with hoods lined in House colours, brown shoes; blazers bound with green and gold braid, navy overcoat; summer dresses (known as sacks) were light green with a cream collar, gold braid sewn onto the shoulders of tunics for deportment; Panama hat worn in summer and felt hat in winter.'

By the late 1950s, the summer uniform had changed to 'green check dresses, panama hats and brown ankle socks' (Rosalind Carreck, 1964). Rosalind also describes the PE uniform, which had replaced the brown overalls: 'white aertex shirt and smart green pleated green shorts and ghastly black woollen swimsuits that shrunk to felt in the open-air pool.'

An early group photo: girls are not wearing a strict uniform at this time.

Mrs Page and the General Sixth, 1960.

Ann Hinds' daughter, Wendy Durrant (Hinds, 1975) recalls that the sweater had changed to 'a fawn sweater with green line at the V neck, later changed to a grey sweater' whilst a 'green cord beret and grey coat (very prickly!)' had replaced the felt hats. The summer dress had also changed to a 'stripy dress in green and white ... and fabric poppered belt'. Wendy writes, 'the sixth form wore tweed skirts until about 1972 when own clothes were allowed, but only skirts'. The PE uniform had also changed: 'yellow sweatshirt, green pleated skirt, green knickers and white aertex shirt for games, with knee-high green socks with yellow stripes for lax'.

Stephanie Gilbert (Thomson, 1979) remembers one particularly controversial rule: 'Having ones hair tied back was one of the many rules that I remember vividly from my junior school years – and if it wasn't appropriately secured one would get sent to the staffroom to collect an infamous elastic band. What constituted "appropriately" always seemed to be open to debate and I remember the solidarity of our class if it was felt the elastic band had been administered inappropriately – everyone in the class would whip out the elastic bands at next break and no matter the length of your hair it would be adorned with numerous bunches sprouting irregularly from the head!'

When Wendy Durrant's daughter, Pippa Wilkins (Durrant, 1999) joined the school, the uniform consisted of 'in Little Saints the winter blouse which was a creamy colour, later changed to a much-preferred green and white striped version. My favourite piece of uniform when I was five was the yellow jumper with the big daisy for PE. I later helped to campaign to change the senior yellow games jumper to a white hooded one for lacrosse. Purse belts were an essential part of the Junior School uniform, where we could store 10p for the emergency phone call home ... We wore a tunic until the end of Junior School when we graduated to a skirt which had to be rolled up many times to ensure it was well above the knee, especially if a trip to Merchant Taylors' was on the cards. The green duffle coat was rarely worn as it wasn't very "cool" so we preferred to freeze instead. For the sixth form we could wear anything we wanted, apart from ripped jeans and a bare midriff.' In the summer, girls wore a green and white striped dress.

Uniform today is very similar to that of the 1990s, although the striped shirt has been replaced by a gingham one, with senior girls wearing a short-sleeved version in the summer months instead of a summer dress.

Pippa Wilkins (Durrant) in the Little St Helen's winter and summer uniforms, late 1980s.

The new Senior School uniform, c.1998.

The 21st Century and a Vision for the Future

Mary Morris

St Helen's began its second century with a new Head, but with the same ethos and qualities that had set it apart from other schools over its first 100 years. The school entered the new millennium as an over-subscribed, successful academic institution. It was described by *The Good Schools Guide* as 'an extraordinarily unsung haven' that is 'forward-looking and cutting edge'. No sooner had the champagne corks popped than the Independent Schools Inspectorate announced their impending visit. The Inspectors noted that 'The school provides a very good quality of education. Very good personal relationships, high expectations and good teaching ensure that girls achieve high academic standards. The school has a strong sense of community in which individuals are well known, valued and supported. The quality of pastoral care is high.' This was a great confirmation of the high standards that have characterised the school since its inception.

New buildings are always an exciting development for any school. The successful Centenary Campaign to build a new swimming pool and sports complex, and provide bursary funds for pupils in hardship, built on the success of 'Bricks Leader'. An excellent team of parent volunteers worked tirelessly to raise money. A Gala Evening with Patricia Hodge at the Merchant Taylors' Livery Hall in the City, the 'Robby Williams' lookalike concert, the Auction of Promises and many pupil activities involved us all in the development of this major new facility. Other improvements to the school were also taking place. The expanded Newell dining room took shape along with a new computer suite and mathematics classrooms. The revamped Quad became home to an armillary sphere sundial donated by the school to celebrate the dedication of the Seldon family, and also the depth of feeling the school has for its Old Girls. It is inscribed with the words of early prospectuses: 'Work not for school, but for life; toil not for time but for eternity' – words as true in 2001 as when first written.

Roger Black with Chairman of the Governors, Rosie Faunch, opening the Sports Hall, December 2006.

(continued on p. 122)

Sport – *Rosie Jackman (Head of PE)*

Tennis outside the new school hall, c.1915.

Physical Education has always played a prominent part in school life. Tennis and swimming have been constant favourites. Hockey and cricket were played in the early days with lacrosse introduced in the early 1920s. Lacrosse and netball are an important part of the curriculum today.

The school has had its fair share of teachers who have been international lacrosse players and in turn has produced international players amongst its pupils, including Wendy Reynolds and Sarah and Rachel Kirchheimer, following in the footsteps of Ann Morton who left St Helen's in 1953 before making it big on the international lacrosse stage. Rachel Kirchheimer (2001), who has been part of the England squad since leaving school, writes, 'When we entered Year 7 St Helen's had had two to three years of fantastic lacrosse results, thanks to the coaching of two international players, Ali Powell and Vic Cranwell ... I remember them playing "good cop/bad cop" to get us motivated and it definitely paid off. Our team remained undefeated until our final match of the season as U15s – we were devastated! A large number of the people I stay in contact with now from school were part of that team and I believe the team spirit developed on the pitch cannot be replicated in the classroom.'

Edwardian girls enjoyed table-tennis and badminton has been popular since the 1980s. The drill parades of the 1900s have

Lacrosse, 1930s (above) and 2000 (below).

been replaced with cross-country running and choreographed movement. Athletics was introduced in 1994, resulting in the annual Senior School Sports Day. St Helen's girls have always danced, though the preferred styles have changed from ballet, to ballroom to street dance, and an annual Gym and Dance

Display, started in 2000, gives 250 girls the chance to perform their own routines.

The choice of sports available continues to grow, and girls in Years 10 and 11 can now choose from a large selection including trampolining, aerobics, golf, volleyball, fitness sessions in the new fitness suite and dance, whilst sixth formers can also opt for self-defence, kick-boxing, table-tennis and Pilates. Academic PE is the most recent addition to the curriculum, with GCSE introduced in 2004, AS Level in 2006 and A2 Level in 2007.

Ski trips continue to be popular with groups taken annually, whilst sports tours are a regular feature. Lacrosse tours have gone to the USA, Australia and Canada and a netball tour went to Malta in May 2007. Sarah Ksirchheimer (1997) recalls, 'The 1995 USA tour really opened our eyes to the playing standard of our opponents, the facilities they had available, and the amount of training that they did. We came back from this tour with a cohesive group of players, all now much more aware of the tactical knowledge

Ski trip, 2009.

required to be a good player.' On all tours, the girls have to train hard and the teams they encounter push players to their limits. However, not only do sports tours raise the standard of play, but the educational experience is exceptional in terms of exposure to other cultures, discipline, commitment, shared experiences and fun.

As the school has grown, so have its sports facilities. The senior gymnasium and squash court was opened in 1976. Unlike the old gym (now the Old Hall) the new gym was light and airy. The forethought and planning that went into the senior gym has paid dividends as it is still heavily used and a pleasure to teach in 33 years on. In December 2006, the new sports hall and dance studio were opened by Olympic silver medallist Roger Black. This facility, together with the new swimming pool, makes up the impressive Sports Centre which has quickly become a focal point, used throughout the day and after school.

Whatever sport has been followed, be it judo or trampolining, the underlying purpose has remained the same; to provide a means to fitness and relaxation, to experience teamwork and to learn to cope with the fun of winning and the disappointment of losing.

Dance, 2007.

The Houses Today – *Paul Tiley (Deputy Head)*

Governor Michael Clark presenting the House Maths Cup, 2007.

The House System is an essential part of the St Helen's experience, enabling older girls to work with, help and support their younger peers through participation in a variety of extra-curricular activities. Over the years it has grown in strength, providing fond and permanent memories.

The girls' sense of House identity has been strengthened with Heads of House and Sixth Form House Captains constantly looking for new and innovative ways of building House spirit. When the girls join Senior School, House polo shirts are now part of the uniform; these are in the House colours with the House badge embroidered onto the chest. The introduction of the role of overall House Co-ordinator has helped the Houses work together to raise funds during House Charity Week for charities related to the annual whole school charity theme. For example, in the academic year beginning 2005 it was the African Initiative.

House Netball, Lacrosse, Rounders, Tennis and Swimming flourish as does Sports Day – one of the highlights of the summer term. House Arts takes over the school towards the end of this term and probably encapsulates the spirit of the House system more than any other event. House Maths is always competitive with the final played out in front of the Senior School at the end of the autumn term. All House events count towards the overall House Championship with points gained for commendations and profile points (and still deducted for sanctions). The winner receives the shield, kindly donated by the PTA in 2005, in a highly charged atmosphere during the last assembly of the academic year.

Sports Day.

The presentation of the armillary sphere sundial to Mary Rose Seldon, watched by girls and Old Girls, 2001.

In 2002 we had an excuse for celebrations as we marked the centenary of the school on this site with exciting plans for the expansion of the school community. In September 2003 the refurbished Little St Helen's opened as Little Gables with our first three year olds, a very welcome addition to the community. Watching over 1,100 girls climb the scaffolding for the most recent whole school photo was a sure indicator of the growth and popularity of the school and a humbling reminder of the responsibility we have to do our best for every girl.

'Looking back on my time at St Helen's fills me with a wistfulness and nostalgia that is only magnified as the years go by ... From the corridors of Claremont to the Sixth Form common room, I will be forever grateful for what the school has done for me: for nurturing once-hidden abilities, for countless memories, life-long friends, and the best spring-board I could have hoped for into my future.'

CHARLOTTE MATALON (2005)

Founder's Day, 2009.

'I remember my first few days at St Helen's vividly – I was one who held the ignorant belief that an all girls' school was one to be entered at peril! However, I was totally wrong. As soon as I found my classroom I was made to feel welcome ... and I made firm friends straight away. Many of my recollections generally involve laughing-so-hard-that-I-cry and watching others laugh-so-hard-that-they-cry. Needless to say, I am thrilled that I chose to change schools as I settled in so quickly.

Victoria Brazier (2009)

It seems that once we do something at St Helen's it is immediately embedded as a tradition. In 2007 the Sports Hall became the venue for the annual Founder's Day Assembly. It is wonderful to be able to meet as a whole school, which I believe has not happened since Miss Leader's day. We now have doughnuts or cookies to celebrate our birthday every year – another tradition that I am sure no future Head will dare to rescind.

The school has always welcomed celebrities to enrich the girls' learning. The highly successful drama workshops with Patricia Hodge and David Suchet inspired many of our budding actresses. Renowned musician David Fanshawe inspired us all to be the two per cent of the people who 'do', as opposed to the 98 per cent of the population who just 'think about it' while Andrew Motion, the Poet Laureate, made us all realise that poetry is part of our everyday life. Ian Rose, Paralympic double medallist, inspired us as did Andrew Cooney, the youngest person to walk to the South Pole. Recently we were privileged to hear the extraordinary stories of how two Gurkha soldiers won the Victoria Cross.

For over 100 years St Helen's has provided a forward-looking education in an intellectually stimulating environment, so the introduction of the International Baccalaureate in 2004, with its focus on all round education within an international perspective, built on what has always been a strong feature of the school. As only the third UK girls' school to become an IBO World School, the move recognised the creative energy of the girls as well as their involvement in the wider community, participation in sport, PHAB, CCF and extra-curricular activities.

So what of the future? The vivid history of this school bears witness to the qualities of the girls and staff that make this a very special community where everyone can chase their dreams and achieve. When Mrs Cadman was honoured with a lifetime award

(continued on p. 128)

Leavers

A relatively new tradition is that of inviting Old Girls to be our Guest of Honour at Speech Day. We have been delighted to welcome back: Baroness Rosalie Wilkins, appointed as a Labour peer in 1999 in the House of Lords with a particular interest in disability; Vanessa Lawrence CB, Director General and Chief Executive of Ordnance Survey; Dame Barbara Mills QC, the first woman to be Director of Public Prosecutions and previous head of the Crown Prosecution Service; Sallyann Keizer, television producer; Puneeta Mongia, management consultant; Luisa Baldini, a reporter for the BBC; Anne Inglesfield, learning and organisational development manager at BP; Caroline Daniel, a journalist for *The Financial Times*; Amanda Calfe, a pilot; and Jo Finburgh, a fundraiser for Friends of the Earth. Their tales of their time in school and life afterwards inspire and entertain our current pupils and give us all a sense of the vibrancy and diversity of the girls who choose to wear green and how they make their mark in society.

An even more recent tradition for today's leavers is the hosting of our Leavers' Ball at a prestigious hotel in London; the marquee, which accommodated the Ball from the late 1990s, is no longer required for Speech Day as we use the Sports Hall.

Our leavers' destinations reflect the wealth and diversity of opportunity that is available to modern women. Medicine is always a popular degree choice amongst our Year 13 leavers, as are dentistry, economics, humanities, sciences and languages. Many choose to take a gap year to travel and work around the world. We look forward to welcoming more of our leavers back as Guests of Honour in years to come!

Leavers' Ball, 2008.

The Changing Curriculum – *Anne Weaver (History teacher and Professional Development Manager)*

The purpose of St Helen's has always been to provide a broad, balanced curriculum which demands that the girls become resourceful, well-informed citizens. To this end, since the school's foundation, the curriculum has covered subjects taught for publicly recognised qualifications, and a variety of topics which develop the knowledge and understanding which are important to becoming a thoughtful and successful member of society. The approach to teaching and learning has changed over the years, but the goal has remained constant.

Public examinations have formed part of what was offered since 1903, when Cambridge examinations were taken, albeit by very few, and 1906, when several girls were successful in Music and Art examinations. The London Matriculation was first sat in 1910, the Higher Matriculation in 1939. Yet this did not usher in a drive to expand the number of formal qualifications. Yearbooks indicate that for the following 20 years, it was not considered necessary for such examinations to dominate education – a profound difference to expectations nowadays.

St Helen's adapted itself to change. In 1964 the Head's report referred to the general sixth form course on offer to girls 'who are not suited for the academic course leading to Advanced level' which suggests that girls and their parents could see value in continuing their education without reference to examinations; by 1984 all girls

in the sixth form sat A levels. Today's success in public examinations ensures that all girls can go on to higher education, should they wish to, and overwhelmingly they do. We hope that the girls who leave us today are inspired to continue their education for the nobler reasons of passion for their subject and love of learning; yet how many now would embark upon study at university, with no prospect of a degree? Girls from St Helen's went to Cambridge in the 1930s, even though that university was not prepared until 1948 to acknowledge women's achievements by awarding them degrees.

Subjects which have been taught throughout the school's life include English, Music, Drama, French, History, Geography, Art and Physical Activity. Methods of teaching have evolved: lectures give way to more interactive, inquiry-based work, but the place of these subjects in a good education has not been questioned. While Mathematics has been offered to everyone, there seems to have been a change in perception of this subject over the decades; Arithmetic, not Mathematics, was taught in Junior School in the 1950s. In 1980, the only CSE offered by the school was for those 'eminently unmathematical souls'. Yet in 2009 over 60 per cent of the sixth form are studying mathematics.

A lesson, c.1931.

The study of foreign languages has been available since 1899. French and Latin were taught in the 1910s and 1920s; German, Ancient Greek and Spanish came later. By the 1990s Russian and Italian could be learnt. Today there are also opportunities in Japanese and Mandarin. Unexamined before and during World War One, language is now an integral part of the International Baccalaureate. Languages studied reflect our place in the global community.

Other subject choices also illustrate changes in society. In the early days of the school, knitting was on the curriculum so that the girls could provide clothing for British soldiers in the Boer War. This gave way in 1939 to millinery, taught as part of housecraft. Domestic studies had been a key part of the teaching since 1935. Cookery and needlework remained available from the 1940s to the 1990s. Mindful of the requirements of employers and the desire to show that St Helen's offered, from 1988, much *more* than the National Curriculum, Design and Technology was introduced in Key Stage 3. In 1983 O Level in computer studies was offered. Seen then as a daring choice made by a few, ICT is of course, embedded in the curriculum today.

Science was taught as Nature Study and through the auspices of the Literary and Scientific society until the late 1920s. It developed to be a strength of the school, with biology, chemistry and physics being taught as separate subjects. Prior to 1985 girls may have chosen only one of the Sciences, after the advent of GCSE all had to be taken at some level. We now have two-thirds of girls in the sixth form studying one or more of the Sciences.

Some Personal, Social, Health and Citizenship Education is taught today in distinct timetabled lessons. This type of education however, is linked to the school's ethos and its most powerful lessons are delivered in our reactions to the daily concerns of the community and its individuals. While timetabled sessions in such matters may not have featured in the early years of the school, this teaching was fundamental to the education of every girl and formed part of Miss Rowland Brown's 'teaching in its widest sense'. For much of the 20th century, emotional and moral education was provided through discussions with the headmistress and her staff, and was emphasised by the range of lectures and charitable

Year 8 independent learning: 'Thinking Outside The Box', 2009.

involvements of the girls. In 1989 an additional perspective was introduced through the 'Way of Life' course with Harrow School. Guest speakers explained their views on ethical issues of the day, and participants met in groups to discuss whatever they wished.

The curriculum continues to include lectures, site visits and debates. The school realises the importance of being knowledgeable about current affairs and of broadening understanding beyond the classroom. A speaker on life in Russia in 1931 described it as 'a country deliberately undergoing hardship in order to speed up industrialisation'. Talks in 1934 covered the work of the League of Nations and the crisis between Italy and Abyssinia. In the 21st century we have had speakers on topics as diverse as the travels of Benedict Allen, Peter Oppenheimer's perspective of the global economy, the life of Helen of Troy and eminent geographer Dr Rex Walford's views on global warming.

Each headmistress devised a curriculum that equips girls to take their places as citizens with confidence. Above all they aim to instil in every girl a love of learning for learning's sake.

Memories of the IB – *Amy Brewer (2006)*

My memories of being one of the first IB students are a bit of a blur. If I call to mind that period in my life I get hit with a wall of facts, images and sound-bites reflecting just how much information we digested.

I like to imagine myself pacing through the corridors like the politicians in 'The West Wing', although in reality I'm sure it was two years of frantic dashing from class to class; from 'Othello' to Mao, ecology to algebra, Descartes to *je ne sais quoi*. Looking back, I have no idea how we managed to cram so much in – I remember being busy all the time, but very happy – with six subjects as well as TOK, CAS, the Group 4 project, an Extended Essay and a normal teenager's social life.

Looking back now, it seems what I'll always remember most is the camaraderie between the 21 girls. From the first day, on our overnight bonding session when we played a disastrous murder mystery game, through our field trips, CAS activities and shared deadlines, to our last day together receiving results, we were a dedicated crew of enthusiastic and high-spirited risk-takers. And that's what the IB demanded.

Today the IB still has an impact on my life. At university I take two 'outside' subjects along with my main degree, but I long to do more. I really enjoyed studying such an array of topics. Luckily for me, nearly all of them have come back to haunt me in varying forms: biology's neuroscience in Psychology, history's Napoleonic wars in History of Art, maths' logic in Semantics.

Throughout my international adventures in the three years since I left school I have learnt that wherever you are in the world, if you mention that you studied the IB in the presence of fellow IB alumni they will invariably cheer, hug and high-five you. It's a great feeling, knowing that the bond we formed also extends worldwide.

I know we finished with the conviction that we'd done something worthwhile and that anything was possible.

First ever IB results, 2006.

from the Teaching Awards Trust, we were all thrilled that her dedication had been recognised and aware that the award was also a symbol of all our teachers' dedication. With such inspirational teaching, girls do seem to really enjoy learning. Lessons now involve whiteboards and the internet, reinforcing the traditional value of academic scholarship and independent learning which stretches from the classroom into the wider world.

St Helen's girls have intellectual curiosity, confidence without arrogance, integrity, and respect for others. They use their talents and enthusiasm for the benefit of the community and develop skills to help them to play a role on the national and international stage. Helping others dates back to the earliest days of the school and this spirit is just as active as ever.

St Helen's has long enjoyed an excellent relationship with Merchant Taylors' School. We all know how much fun and how important it is to share activities with the boys, whether it be volleyball, the Leavers' Ball, plays, sport, music, PHAB or CCF. These activities broaden horizons and the academic and extra-curricular activities enrich the life of both schools.

I am enormously proud of St Helen's girls. They take intellectual risks, approach unfamiliar situations and uncertainty with courage and forethought, and have the independence of spirit to explore new ideas and strategies. They understand the importance of academic, physical and emotional balance to achieve personal well-being. Knowledgeable young women, they explore ideas and issues, use their initiative to think critically and creatively, and make reasoned, ethical decisions. They are

'I realised that I wanted to come back for sixth form, five years after leaving in 2002. The first day back, after my extended leave, I was late! This has only happened twice since, both very important days ...

I was completely surprised at having made the short list for prefects, and was sure I would never make the team, but I still wanted to be at school when the final list was revealed. This day was to be made interesting by the fact that road works were to start on this day, on my coach route to school. I arrived at school just in time for assembly, but almost 30 minutes late to find out the new prefect team. On my way to sign in, I was met by Mrs Morris. Shocked is the only way to describe how I felt when I was told that I was to be Junior School Prefect. Having convinced myself that this could never happen, I couldn't even take in the list, to see who else had made the final cut. This was my second late, another important day.

The only day I was late since, was the morning of my statistic's 1 module. This was again due to traffic ... There was another girl on my coach in the same situation, and it is fair to say that we became slightly hysterical as the minutes ticked by. We only missed the start of the exam by 10 minutes, but I am sure our stress levels had not been helped by the journey to school.

Happily, my coach has yet to be late again, but I am sure that the next time it is, will once again be an important day.'

ROSIE GORDON (2009)

Language lesson, 2005.

The Badge

'*in hoc vincite velut illi crescite*'
'Conquer by the cross and grow like the daisies'
Literal: 'In this (cross) conquer and grow like them (daisies).'

The *cross* is central to the badge of St Helen's, being associated with our patron saint, Helena of Constantinople. Helena was born in obscurity before becoming the wife of Constantius, an ambitious officer. Their son, Constantine, became Christian Roman emperor.

During Constantine's rule there were rival claimants to his imperial power, making a battle inevitable. The first part of the school motto, '*In hoc vincite*,' refers to a vision that Constantine had just before the Battle of Milvian Bridge in A.D. 312.

While marching towards the battle at noon, Constantine (till then a devotee of the Sun God) saw a cross of light centred on the sun, carrying the motto, in Greek letters, 'In this (sign) conquer'.

That night Constantine had a dream in which Christ appeared to explain the labarum, or Chi-Rho sign, and told him to use it as a standard with which to defend his army. The sign is constituted from the first two Greek letters of the word meaning anointed, Christ.

Constantine ordered his soldiers to paint the sign on their shields. Later that day they obtained victory.

Helena was closely associated with the cross on which Jesus gave his life and, at 75, led a party to Jerusalem to find the holy relic. Excavations on a site indicated by local Christians found three different crosses. Helena declared that the cross that healed a terminally ill woman must be that on which Christ had been crucified. On the spot, Helena built the Church of the Resurrection, the holiest of all Christian sites.

Helena returned to Rome, bringing with her large parts of the True Cross for veneration. She is considered by Orthodox and Roman Catholic Churches as Equal to the Apostles, and patron of archaeologists.

Although the daisies of the school badge which flank the cross are usually taken as illustrating the flowers of the school fields, the words '*velut illi crescite*' (grow like them) indicates that their presence is more than simply decorative.

The name, daisy, may be a corruption of 'day's eye' because of the flowers' habit of opening to the light. Daisies welcome the light of Constantine's vision and suggest openness to enlightenment – education's goal.

Daisies have been described as: 'cheerful and exuberant … rarely looking out of place in our beds and borders … having distinctive personalities.' Flowers with such characteristics seem appropriate for the badge of such a diverse and lively community.

A Sixth Form lesson, 2009.

The Daisy Story –
Rebecca Hershman (Baxter, 1964)

Mrs Garrett opened her first 'High School' in Chester Road in 1899 but soon needed larger buildings and more space. She found a plot of land for sale on the corner of Eastbury Road and Carew Road.

It is hard for us to imagine today that this site was countryside and the plot she found was a rough field. The corner site and surrounding fields were a mass of ox-eye daisies and she never forgot the wonderful carpet of yellow and white. Mrs Garrett hoped her new school would flourish and grow like the strong and beautiful wild flowers she could see all around her. When the new school building was opened in May 1902 she called it St Helen's, to please her much-loved and respected mother, who loved the church of the same name in Bishopsgate.

She created a school crest, which we all wear on our blazers today, and the ox-eye daisy that was 'so essentially a Northwood plant' was included. The pure white and the rich gold of the ox-eye daisy represented the values Mrs Garrett wanted to encourage. She saw the golden heart of the daisy as the school and the array of white petals as the pupils. Each would play their part within the school community, and as the parts of the flower helped create the whole, so the pupils, together with their teachers, would do the same. She realised too that if one petal of a daisy was damaged, or if one pupil within the school seriously misbehaved then – just like the daisy – so the school would be damaged and spoilt. She envisaged a community supporting and caring for each other and hoped that everyone connected with the growth of St Helen's would strive to achieve the same aims and values in education and personal behaviour. It was a simple concept but she knew it was one that would need hard work and patience from all involved.

Our aims today are just the same. We all try to contribute to school life by working hard and joining in with each other. We are like petals of the daisy. Each one of us is a valuable part of St Helen's – we too are trying to achieve the simplicity and the beauty of the daisy.

confident and creative and willingly collaborate. They are open to the perspectives, values and traditions of others and demonstrate their personal commitment to make a positive difference to those around them and to the environment.

The most recent Inspection Report in 2007 is not so different from that written 90 years earlier in 1919 which judged that 'development of character, of resourcefulness and of the power of managing others are marked features of the work of the school'. I am sure many parents of today's pupils would agree with this sentiment. The Inspectors concluded that, 'This is a school that knows where it is going, and how it intends to get there'. I believe this has always characterised this extraordinary school. Our ethos is still rooted in May Rowland Brown's vision, but developed, strengthened and moved on by so many charismatic and committed staff since. The 2007 judgement that: 'This is a highly successful school ... with courteous, hard-working and well-rounded girls of integrity and independence' is testament to 110 years of dedication and innovation and a perfect springboard for the challenges that the future holds.

'I think the most unique thing about St Helen's is that we are not moulded to become the cleverest, sportiest or most artistic students, but just given that extra bit of help we need to find our own talents, to bring us that much closer to becoming the type of person we want to be. The teachers here definitely recognise and embrace our individuality and I think that's what makes St Helen's different to any other school; teachers here don't give you all the answers, but they will always make sure you find the answer yourselves ... Whether it's dressing in pyjamas for mufti day, running around the common room looking for blue face paint for Shackleton House Netball, it's just so much fun to be doing it together with your closest friends.'

KRISHMA SANGANI (CURRENT PUPIL)

Little St Helen's Today – *Joanna Chaventré (Head of Little St Helen's)*

My first memory of Little St Helen's was on my assessment day when I wore a blue dress with a large daisy on the front. I have many memories of my time in LSH but they are mainly of having great fun and happy times. I returned to LSH as Mrs Gosling's Prefect, helping to organise the sixth formers who eagerly wanted to help the 'little ones'. I desperately wanted to teach myself so sat avidly watching Mrs Gosling, trying to learn as much as I could. My dream of becoming a teacher became true when, in September 2002, I joined the staff.

I began my professional career at LSH teaching Reception in Gables. Mrs Gosling retired in July 2003 and I became involved in another phase of LSH as the new Nursery began in September 2003 and the intake increased from two to three forms, and I became Deputy Head of the Foundation Stage. Little Gables was officially opened on 17th November 2003 by Rosie Faunch, the Chairman of Governors. In December 2005 it was announced that I was to be the new Head of LSH from the Summer Term of 2006.

Little St Helen's is now accommodated in two charming houses, Gables and Little Gables. Little Gables accommodates children in the Foundation Stage. Gables is the Key Stage 1 building where Year 1 and Year 2 are situated. There is an excellent purpose-built gymnasium and two multi-purpose halls which can be used for music and drama activities. Each classroom has its own computers and interactive whiteboard and there are two extensive libraries. The library in Little Gables is called the Gosling Library after LSH's former Head.

The girls receive close personal attention from specialised staff and maintain close links with girls further up the school. LSH is still allocated their own Prefect and older girls continue to support the younger pupils in their learning. We believe that each child should be treated as an individual and given every opportunity to develop her talents and abilities to the full. Each class has a

A Nursery class, 2007.

Carousel music lesson, 2009.

dedicated teaching assistant and specialist staff offer music, French, physical education, speech and drama, ballet, dance and origami, adding an extra dimension to the teaching.

Lunch is compulsory for all and considered to be part of the curriculum. It takes place in the Gables dining room and the Year 2 children still take on the responsibility of being the servers and helpers. The Nursery and Reception girls walk to Gables for their lunch and boaters continue to be worn with pride by the girls. There are no animals kept but if you ask the girls they all know that Miss Chaventré's favourite animal is a dog. There are plenty of toys

Little St Helen's girls reading, c.2007.

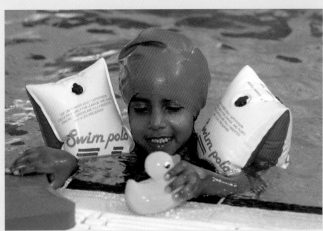

Nursery swimming lesson, 2007.

the girls can play with in the playground. The grounds continue to be used extensively, stories are read under the shade sails, 'pink magic' has been replaced with 'magic water', and lessons in literacy play a major part in the curriculum.

Now when I see prospective parents I am often asked how long I have been at the school, a question that always takes me some time to answer.

Girls playing in the Little Gables playground, 2009.

Junior School Today – *Kathy Serinturk (Head of Junior School)*

As I look out of my office window a kaleidoscope of pink spreads across the playground. I put on my wings and cape before going into the playground. It's Fairy Day for Year 3 and there is excitement in the air. As I am joined by a tall mermaid, I smile to myself; at what other place of work can you arrive wearing wings and not be out of place? But there is a serious side; Fairy Day is Year 3's introduction to independent learning, enjoying a day of 'Active Learning' where they will create, criticise, evaluate and make decisions. Active Learning is an important part of the Junior School curriculum today, and the essence of learning.

Fairy Day usually takes place at the end of the spring term, and has become a tradition. Another tradition, started during my time as Head, is the Indian Market – active learning at its best. The planning is handed over to the girls and they look at ways to raise money to help schools in India. They make Indian food, jewellery and trinkets. Girls lay out colourful rugs to sit on, light joss sticks, play Indian music and they make hundreds of pounds. Junior School enjoys raising money and girls regularly turn up at my door asking to organise a fund-raising event.

In the past many of our residential trips took place in the spring term, but we had to change this when the girls sleeping on the *Golden Hinde* in March, experiencing life as Tudor sailors, spent the night on a draughty deck in the snow! They survived, but more importantly learnt first-hand about the grueling life of the Tudor sailor.

There have been many residential trips over the years to Swanage, Welsh Bicknor, the Isle of Wight, and, more recently, Cuffley Camp and Cromer. These have all been great fun and a huge learning experience. On the trip to Welsh Bicknor the girls visited the mine. Gillian Furphy, a class teacher since 1980 recalls, 'When you got out at the bottom you often felt a couple of hands grab yours in the pitchy blackness and say, "It's a bit dark Miss Furphy, you might not like it!". And their fear was well-founded, the pit was so black you could only see your group, the one in

Mrs Kathy Serinturk reading with Junior School girls.

front of you had disappeared into the blackness, it was scary and exhilarating and all done without a risk assessment!'

Spring is also a time when nature wakes up. Mrs Botten, PA to the Junior Head, who has worked at St Helen's since 1983, remembers: 'Several years ago, every spring, the JS pond was visited by the drake from HMS *Warrior* and his duck lady friend. They would wander up and down the paths and sometimes chill out on the Science Department pond. Then the ducklings were born and they would join their parents strolling round the grounds and causing great delight to the girls and staff alike ... Unfortunately, they have not been seen for a few years now, but will be fondly remembered by many.'

Autumn is the start of the new school year, crisp new uniforms, shiny shoes, sharpened pencils. Year 3 are met by their Year 6 buddies, who look after them in their first week and before long Year 3 are confident little girls eager to learn.

Junior School is always evolving but the values and atmosphere stay the same. Visitors say it is a vibrant and happy place. When I came for my interview I remember Mrs Mary Morris saying to me, 'there is a certain atmosphere here that you can't quite put your

An art lesson, 2009.

finger on: it is unique. If I could bottle it I'd make a fortune,' and she is right.

Summer is the busiest term, jam-packed with events: the Year 6 play, prize-giving, reports, residential trips, lessons often taught outside to make use of our beautiful grounds.

Prize-giving is a very prestigious affair; it is a time when we award our pupils and showcase our music and drama, but it is a fairly new development, begun while Christine Thorbourne was Head. The guest speaker is always an Old Girl. One of my saddest prize-givings was when I had to say goodbye to my deputy, Mrs Joy Williamson, who was retiring. She was my first deputy and we had worked together for three great years.

Mrs Williamson recalls: 'I was only going to stay for five years: at least that's what I planned. I stayed 15 years! What made me stay so long? Mainly that indefinable atmosphere that is "St Helen's". A sense of history, a sense of purpose, a sense of being where it's happening but most of all that sense of community, friendship and fellowship, of working together for a common purpose.

What do I remember? The obvious things, of course: the centenary celebrations, singing in the joint choral society concerts, prize-giving, Speech Days and Founder's Days, Junior School Sports Days and Swimming Galas, Christmas productions and the incredible opportunities there were for the girls ... But also the smaller things: helping a pupil to overcome her fear of dogs during

a trip to Swanage; "Water Week" and visiting the Canal Museum, pond-dipping and driving down to the South Coast and paddling in a freezing cold sea; tea and toast with Kathy after school, while we chewed over the day and, above all, the people.'

Art and music have always been strong in Junior School and this continues today. The walls are hung with huge canvasses painted by girls.

Junior School is a place of opportunities, for having a go, trying new things out. It is a place of celebration and achievement. We have a fortnightly celebration assembly where the girls receive stickers or certificates for work well done. We have 'The Little Miss Awards' at the end of each term to award those girls who are conscientious, organised, friendly, creative or who have made big progress. We also have Head Teacher's Awards which girls receive for outstanding pieces of work.

When I took over as Head I was lucky to have a secure school with high academic standards. I was immensely indebted to the hard work of others before me and I started with very strong foundations on which to continue to build. Junior School is and always has been a vibrant community, one with academic excellence, where every pupil is prepared to take risks and enjoys the challenge.

'My main memory is of that snowy day in the winter of 2006. I have two sisters at St Helen's and we all reluctantly plodded into school ... I knew some of my friends wouldn't be at school, and really, wanted to stay at home curled up on the sofa! But when I arrived, I realised how glad I was to be there. That's the thing with St Helen's – when you are there with your friends and the teachers, it's like the best club in the world.

After a motivational talk from Mrs Serinturk (she rocks at those!) we all went with a will to our classrooms and did snow-themed lessons ... We continued to learn, even in the less-than-ideal conditions and did it with a twist of fun! And to round off a morning of freezing cold excitement, everyone bundled outside to play in the snow.'

FELICITY WAREING (CURRENT PUPIL)

A Vision for the Future – *Lauren Berg (Head Girl, 2009)*

St Helen's is constantly updating to be at the forefront of social and technical progression.

Over the past century we have grown, with society, to become a more ethnically diverse and culturally exciting place to learn, where issues are debated inclusive of a wide range of views, extending our scope to understand and connect. This is something I am certain will be pivotal as we move into the next decade.

I also suspect St Helen's will expand its global networks. The inclusion of Mandarin and Japanese in the curriculum and the school's status as an IBO World School are signs of how eagerly it has embraced the 'shrinking' nature of our world. I have no doubt that in the coming years our links internationally will be strengthened and extended.

The future St Helen's will aim to be environmentally-conscious and live up to our favourite quality and colour: green. With the efforts of the newly established Eco-Club and the introduction of other initiatives, St Helen's is competing for the Eco Schools Green Flag Award. Perhaps in 50 years Old Girls will return to visit a school with solar-panelled roofing and a home-grown lunch menu.

Despite all that has changed as St Helen's has grown, the central ethos has remained. The tradition of being active within the school community is strong, as is the pro-active nature of girls when it comes to sharing their personal interests with each other, and promoting causes they feel motivated by. In my opinion, it is this eagerness to share and engage that feeds the spirit of St Helen's.

As this book assures, fundamental aspects of St Helen's have lived and grown over the past 110 years, constant throughout, and will continue to flourish. St Helen's will, as it always has done, produce women with social, creative and intellectual skills to push the boundaries of success – the girls in green of which I am proud to be one.

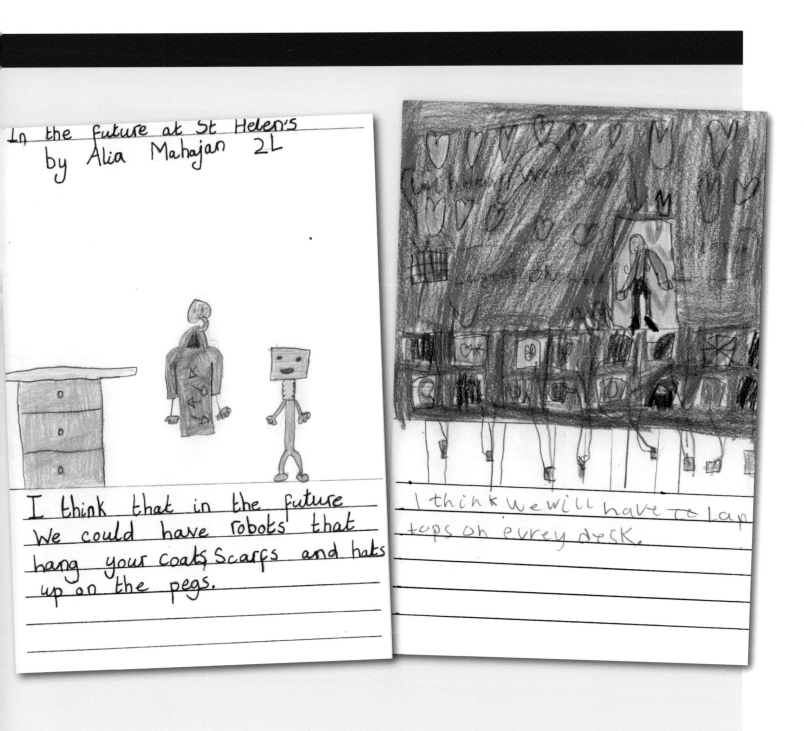

In the future at St Helen's
by Alia Mahajan 2L

I think that in the future We could have robots that hang your coats scarfs and hats up on the pegs.

I think We will have To Lap tops on evrey desk.

A Vision for the Future

The future at St. Helens
By Hannah Wood 2S

What do you want to read

A book that speeks
you just pick up a book.
The book says what do you
want to read.

'In the Future' at St Helen's
By Neha Beri 2L

I went to India.

When you write you say what you
want to write and the pencil writes
it for you

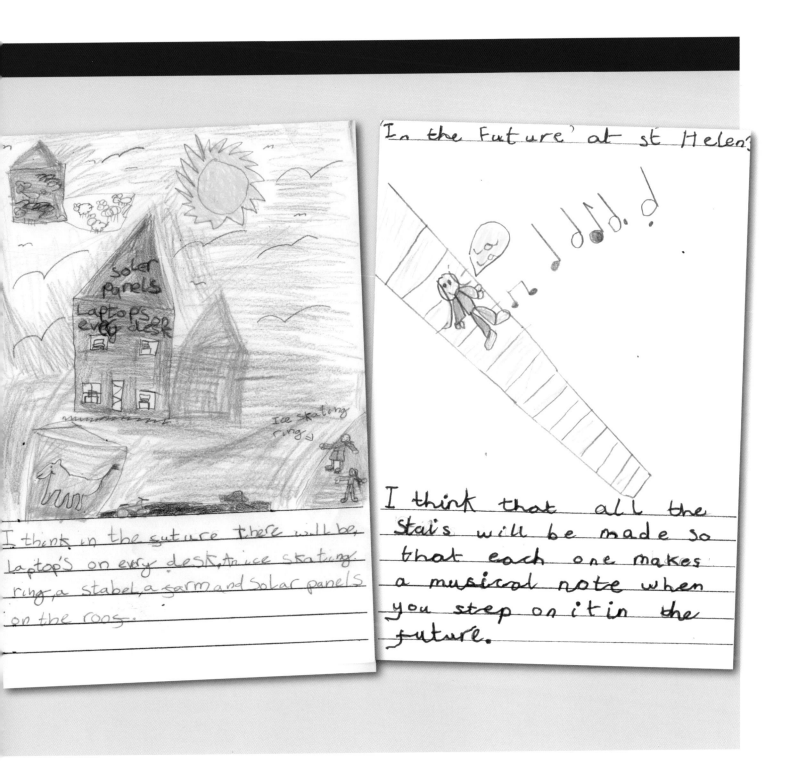

I think in the future there will be laptop's on every desk, An ice skating ring, a stabel, a farm and solar panels on the roof.

'In the Future' at st Helen?

I think that all the stairs will be made so that each one makes a musical note when you step on it in the future.

List of Subscribers

This book has been made possible through
the generosity of the following subscribers:

Emma Abell
Bethanie Abrahams
Chloe Abrahams
Margaret Adam
Emma Dirken Adebayo
Feyi and Ope Adegbite
Ellie Alexander
Afifah Ali
Sabah Ali
Mr Paul N. Anderson
Monica Anson-Tsang
Anushka Asodaria
Priyanka Asodaria
Sarah Asquith
Mary M. Aston
Joan M.C. Baillie
Saachi Bajaj
Harriet May Baptiste
Beverley J. Barnett
Margaret Barrie
Sarah A. Bater
Jenny Beer
Lauren Berg
Natasha Bernard
Kate Berven
Teresa Betts

Abilasha Bhohi
Amrita Bhohi
Rachel Bird (Mellows)
Vanessa Bird (Greaney)
Emma Bloomfield
Rebecca Boardley (now Boyd)
Anna Bockris
Judith Botten
Olivia Jane Boylan
Marilyn Brackley (Dodson)
Mrs S. Bradfield
Molly Bradley-Kidd (Robson)
Victoria Brazier
Tiffany Brenninkmeijer (Jolowicz)
Mrs Joan Brooks (Vermeylen)
Diana Brown (Mills)
Jaime Brown
Miss Maria Brown
Alison Bruce
Susan Bruce
Nancy Buck (Taylor)
Margaret Bunford
Eleanor and Louise Burling
Charlotte Caine
Amanda Jan Calfe
Philippa Carling

Alice Carter
Thalia Cassimatis
Tansy Venetia Castledine
Michelle Cathcart
Andrea Cawthorne (Croad)
Mrs B.S. Champion
Gaby Chan
Lucy S. Chandler
Joanne Chang
Alexandra Chatzidakis (Slaney)
Joanna Chaventré
David Chivers
Dr Keiko Clarence-Smith
Melissa Alexandria Clark
Michael Clark
Tammy Clark
Francesca Clarke
Hana Nicola Clements
Anne Coburn (Brown)
Sophie Cohen
Catherine Coleman (Gill)
Mrs L. Collyear
Julia Conboy (Loosley)
Georgina and Annabel Connah
Helena Connolly
Bella Constantine
Amy and Beth Cook
Jada Cooke
Tia Cooke
Lucy Cooper
Ali Cork (Erskine)
Isobel Cotterell

Jane Coverdale (Riddelsdell)
Mrs V.J.E. Cowley
Rowena Louise Cox
Sandra Crawford (Cole)
Penny Crocker
Lorna Croft
Marilyn Croft (Puttock)
Diana Crowe (Lines)
Jean Crump (Lermit)
Jill Cruse (Haggis)
Dr A. Curtis
Caroline da Costa
Liz Dain
Caroline Daniel
Sarah Daniel
Jan Davies
Mary Davies (Powell)
Lehana De Silva
Jennifer Dee (Couch)
Fiona Dewey
Ridhi P. Dhamecha
Sally Dinwiddie (Croydon)
Celia Dipple
Isabelle Dipple
Madeline Dipple
Helen Dokelman
Mrs Diana C. Dolan
Ann Doubal (Patterson)
Nirvana Douglas
D.J. Dowling
Tegan Drew
Wendy Durrant (Hinds)

Alicia Eames
Miss Margaret Eaton
Rachel Edwards
Victoria Edwards
Anifsa Ershova
Lucy Evans
Rosie Faunch
Catherine Fasanmi
Rosalind Fell
Rosemary Fenn (Clarke)
Lesley Fensom (Askew)
Mrs Pat Fenwick
Kim Fishman
Alex Flash
Sally Fleming (Pollott)
Irene Fotheringham (Scott)
Imogen Franks
Jean Fryer
Nicola K. Gale
Caroline Gardner
Janet Garton
Sally George
Malika Giles
Sara Giles
Aura Gleeson
Moyra Glover (Paulin)
Mrs Jane Gordon (Simmons)
Gina Gosling
Sarah Grace (Lachlan)
Gillian Graper
Michael and Susan Gregory
Annabelle Grenville-Mathers

Hannah Griffiths
Eleanor Grace Grimes
Mrs Minnie Grive
Jennifer Gwyther
Evelyna Hadass
Elizabeth Hall
Jennifer Hamilton
Susan Hamlyn
Neeva Haria
Anthea Hartley
Pat Hatchett
Mrs Judy Hay
Pamela Mary Hayes
Charlotte Haynes
Sarah Haywood
Kate Henderson
Alana Grace Herbert
Alice Herring
Susan Hewitt (Wilson)
Janet Hilken (Sewell)
Gillian Hill
Mrs L.S. Hills
Lisa Hoelscher (Chapman)
Mrs Diana Hollis (Harper)
Sophia Hoschar
Kate Houston
Adele Hughes
Lucy Hughes
Sally Hunt (Nicholls)
Mrs Jean Ide (Whittle)
Jan-Chidi Ikuobase
Natasha Inow

Valerie Isham
Joanna S. James (Young)
Christine Janis
Karina Jayawant
Stephanie Joels
Sarah Johnson Michaelis
Dr Barbara L. Jones
Rosie Joslin
Miriam Kaltz
Vanessa Paula Kanesanathan
Dr Laila Kapadia
Charlotte Kaplan
Dr S. King
Fiona Kingsley Brown
Janet Kirchheimer (Ritchie)
Claire Knust
Alexandra and Anna Kordo
Mrs K.A. Kramer
Emily Krimholtz
Raj Kumar
Emily Kyte
Sophie Ladha
Sarah Laimo (Dowler)
Richard J. Lambert
Lynda Landsman
Charlotte E. Lane
Evelyne Lasar-Lewandowski
Sophie Lassman
Mimi Law
Joanna Lawlor (Twining)
Angela Lawrence
Dr Vanessa Lawrence CB

Jacquie Lawson (Forsyth)
June Leader
Miss M.J. Leaf
Miss Clare Lehovsky
Geraldine Leighton (King)
Jenny Wigan Levejac
Natasha and Lauren Levin
Deirdre Lewis (Brennan)
Jacqui Lewis
Melissa Jane Lewis
Alexandra Liddle
Mrs A.F. Liddell
Mrs Mary Liechti (Wetter)
Loewe Yin Lim
Amanda Little (Jacobson)
Gill Liu
Betty Macadam (McCracken)
Moira Macara
Mrs K.E. MacAuslan
Shelley MacDonald (Nunn)
Jaanki Majithia
Mrs A. Makis
Jacqueline Man
S. Manji
Chloe Marks
Hayley Marks
Ursula Marsden
Penny Marshall
Isabel Mattick
Johanna Mattick
Miss Laura McCullough
Miss Pippa McCullough

Mrs Sheila McCullough (Overend)

Rosemary McLure (Mardon)

Olivia McNulty

Pat McPhail (now Cruddas)

Isobel McVey

Helen Mealins (Cottam)

Francesca Mendola

Clarissa Milkowski

Kim Milkowski

Kirsty Millar (Stevenson)

Olivia Millet

Mrs C. Mollart

Caroline Molyneux

Louise A. Molyneux (Bater)

Yasmin Moore

Ellie Morgan

Mary Morris

Mrs Joanna Morrison

Rosie Morrison

Mrs N. Mownah

Simran-Lily K. Mudhar

Caroline Mundy (Whittle)

Amelia Murphy

Sheila Nash

Nour Nawar

Amber Ndirika

Ruby Ndirika

Mrs B.J. Newcombe

Irenee Nicholas

Susan Northcott

Rosemary O'Boyle-Kelly (Parkes)

Kate Ogden

Olamide Oshunniyi

Ann Oxholm (Powell)

Nevber Öztürk

Ann Page (Dodd)

Lynn Paiba

Anita Patel

Ella Anaya Patel

Ella Patel

Priyal Patel

Ria Patel

Shailesh C. Patel

Ishani Patwal

Miss Sheila Pawson

Julie Perkins (MacFarlane)

Phyllis Pettiford

Abbie Phillips

Nathalie Phillips

Annik Pillaire

Keya Pindolia

Gabriella Pistol

Ellie Pitcher

Harriet Pitcher

Sophie Pitcher

Jane Pollard

Siaan Popat

Carolyn Prendergast (Giddings)

Jane Pudge (Jackson)

Charlotte Quereshi

L.E. Radley

Patricia Raikes

Alyson Rainey (Evans)

Dr Farah Ramjohn

Mrs A.G. Ramsay
J.I. Ranson (Bruce)
Juliette Ratcliff
Angela Redington (Walker)
Elma Reed (Young)
Philippa Reid (Harvey)
Wendy Reynolds
Mrs Gaynor Richardson (Sharp)
Hilary Richardson (Burgess)
Jan Richardson
Julia Richardson (Clements)
Tamsin Rimmer
Joan Roberts (Goodwin)
Sue Roberts (Watkins)
Alison Robinson (Onians)
Helen Niniane Robinson
Isobel Robinson
Natasha Rodikis Presvytis
Jo-Ann Rogers (Eastman)
Dr Ingrid Roscoe
Anna Rowan
Terry Roydon
Emily Rudge
Lis Rushton (Brandon)
Catriona Russell
Mrs D. Salathiel
K. Sammes
Diana Sampson (now Roberts)
Donya Sanders
The Sandom Girls
Ingrid Sandom
Krishma Sangani

Jessica Sargent
Sophie Scholl
Cora A. Schomburg
Antonia Scott (del Tufo)
Lesley Scott
Mrs Kathy Serinturk
Anita Shah
Sajni Shah
Mrs M.L. Shannon
Mrs Helen E. Shepard
Kaira Shetty
Tania Shetty
Poonam Shukla
Sonia Smith (Snow)
Mrs C. Smithers
Shannon K. Smyth
Fiona Snell (Johns)
Jhansi Somapalan
Amber Speed
Elizabeth Speed
R.M. Speirs
Gill Staley (Oakley)
Stallard Family
C. Stephens
Janet Stephenson (Connell)
Lesley Stoppard (Wilkes)
Sarah Stovold
Jill Stredwick (Hewett)
Hannah Summers
Christine Swindlehurst
Magdalena Szafaryn
Miss Catherine Ramirez Tadena

Miss Beryl Taylor
Helena Theo
Jennifer Thomas
Mrs J. Thomas (Miss Ayre)
Anna Talia Thompson
Stephanie Thomson
Katie Tidmarsh
Sally Tucker (Joynson Cork)
Annabel Turner
Coral A. Twaite (Smith)
Ann Twining
Bob Ukiah
Elizabeth Valentine (Cornish)
Katie Vials
Catherine Vick
Anoushka and Aleena Walia
Barbara A. Wallen
Amy Walter
Katherine Walter
Clara Wan
Emily Warburton
Catherine Ward
Jane Wareing (Humphrey)
Jennifer Warren (Bennetts)
Mrs Ann Watson
Penny J. Watson (Archer)
Charlotte Weatherilt
Anne Weaver
Mrs Judith Weedon

Amy, Ellen and Molly Weerasekera
Sally Wells (Collings)
Dinah West (Conington)
Katie West
Deborah Whalley
Matthew Whalley
Rachel Whalley
Lara Whistler
Mrs Marie Williams
Georgia Willis
Mrs Alison J. Wilson
Laura Wilson
Wendy Wilson
Ann Winfield (Montgomery)
Mrs P. Witterick
Vivian Wong Wing Man
Hannah Louise Mary Wood
Isobel Wood (Thorpe)
Mrs Halina Wooldridge
Suzi Woolfson
Miss Elizabeth Worth
Rev. Sally J. Wright (Precious)
Louise Sarah Wyatt
Ms Riya Wykes
Anne Wyman
Felicity Yuille (West)
Nina Zietman
Zoe Zietman

Index of Names and Topics

*'That's the thing with St Helen's – when you
are there with your friends and the teacher,
it's like the best club in the world.'*

FELICITY WAREING (CURRENT PUPIL)